Butterworths New Law Guides

The Freedom of Information Act

2

3 1

2

Butterworths New Law Guides

The Freedom of Information Act 2000

Michael Supperstone QC, MA, BCL
Bencher of the Middle Temple, Deputy High
Court Judge and Recorder of the Crown Court
Timothy Pitt-Payne, BA, BCL, Barrister

both of 11 King's Bench Walk Chambers

Butterworths
LexisNexis™

Members of the LexisNexis Group worldwide

United Kingdom	Butterworths Tolley, a Division of Reed Elsevier (UK) Ltd, Halsbury House, 35 Chancery Lane, LONDON, WC2A 1EL, and 4 Hill Street, EDINBURGH EH2 3JZ
Argentina	Abeledo Perrot, Jurisprudencia Argentina and Depalma, BUENOS AIRES
Australia	Butterworths, a Division of Reed International Books Australia Pty Ltd, CHATSWOOD, New South Wales
Austria	ARD Betriebsdienst and Verlag Orac, VIENNA
Canada	Butterworths Canada Ltd, MARKHAM, Ontario
Chile	Publitecsa and Conosur Ltda, SANTIAGO DE CHILE
Czech Republic	Orac sro, PRAGUE
France	Editions du Juris-Classeur SA, PARIS
Hong Kong	Butterworths Asia (Hong Kong), HONG KONG
Hungary	Hvg Orac, BUDAPEST
India	Butterworths India, NEW DELHI
Ireland	Butterworths (Ireland) Ltd, DUBLIN
Italy	Giuffré, MILAN
Malaysia	Malayan Law Journal Sdn Bhd, KUALA LUMPUR
New Zealand	Butterworths of New Zealand, WELLINGTON
Poland	Wydawnictwa Prawnicze PWN, WARSAW
Singapore	Butterworths Asia, SINGAPORE
South Africa	Butterworths Publishers (Pty) Ltd, DURBAN
Switzerland	Stämpfli Verlag AG, BERNE
USA	LexisNexis, DAYTON, Ohio

A CIP Catalogue record for this book is available from the British Library.

Michael Supperstone and Timothy Pitt-Payne have asserted their rights under the Copyrights, Designs and Patents Act 1988 to be identified as the authors of this work.

ISBN 0 406 93145 3

Printed and bound in Great Britain by Antony Rowe Ltd, Chippenham, Wilts.

Visit Butterworths LexisNexis *direct* at www.butterworths.com

Preface

In 1822 President James Madison, then Chairman of the committee which drafted the First Amendment to the US Constitution, observed—

> "Knowledge will for ever govern ignorance, and a people who mean to be their own governors, must arm themselves with the power knowledge gives. A popular government without popular information or the means of acquiring it, is but a prologue to a farce or a tragedy or perhaps both."

> (Letter sent from Madison to W.T. Barry, 4th August 1822 in Padover (ed) *The Complete Madison* (1953) p 377)

It took almost 150 years for the US to introduce federal freedom of information legislation. Thereafter many other countries followed suit, including Canada, New Zealand, Australia, France, and the Republic of Ireland. In 2000, three years after the election of a Labour Government, freedom of information legislation was enacted in the UK.

Reading the long list of exemptions in the Freedom of Information Act, the spirit of James Madison seems to be little in evidence. Rather, one is reminded of the words of Uncle Clam (of the diplomatic service) in the 1950s musical *Salad Days*—

> "All that my job appeared to consist of
> Much to my chagrin and dismay
> Was a painfully comprehensive list
> Of things I must never do or say."

Nevertheless, this legislation is an important first step along the road to providing a general right of access to information held by public authorities in the UK. Although the Act will not be fully in effect until January 2005, some aspects are already in force. The provisions in relation to publication schemes will come into effect as regards central government within the next 12 months, and will be fully in force by June 2004. It is plainly important for public authorities to prepare for full implementation.

To enable readers of this book to keep up to date, the secondary legislation and other relevant material will be accessible on the Butterworths website; see inside front cover for details.

The necessary password is—freedom

Finally we would like to express our thanks to the editorial staff at Butterworths for their encouragement, patience and hard work, and to colleagues at 11 King's Bench Walk Chambers with whom we have discussed the subject-matter of this book. Usual disclaimers apply.

Michael Supperstone QC
Timothy Pitt-Payne

November 2001

Contents

Table of Statutes

Table of statutes

1 Introduction

BACKGROUND

1.1 The Freedom of Information Act 2000 (FOIA 2000) received royal assent on 30 November 2000.

1.2 The Act had a long and difficult gestation period. The Labour government, elected in May 1997, had included in its manifesto a promise to introduce a Freedom of Information Act. A White Paper 'Your Right to Know',[1] setting out the government's proposals for legislation, was published in December 1997. It was not, however, until May 1999 that the government published a draft Freedom of Information Bill.[2] The Bill was finally introduced into the House of Commons in December 1999. On 7 December 1999, in introducing the Second Reading of the FOI Bill in the House of Commons, the Home Secretary (Mr Jack Straw) stated—

> 'Moreover, the Bill will not only provide legal rights for the public and place legal duties on Ministers and public authorities, but will help to transform the culture of Government from one of secrecy to one of openness. It will transform the default setting from "this should be kept quiet unless" to "this should be published unless". By doing so, public confidence in the processes of government should be raised, and the quality of decision making by the government enhanced'.[3]

[1] Cm 3818 (December 1997).
[2] The draft Bill was published as part of a consultation paper (Cm 4355) on 24 May 1999.
[3] HC 2R, 7 December 1999, col 714.

1.3 At the time of writing the majority of FOIA 2000 is not in force.[1] In particular, the central element of FOIA 2000—the entitlement of a person to receive information from a public body on request—has not come into effect. The Act itself provides that it is to come into force in its entirety at the end of the period of five years beginning with the day on which it was passed, or on such earlier date as the Secretary of State may appoint (s 87(3)). Thus, FOIA 2000 must be fully implemented, at the latest, by 30 November 2005.

[1] As to commencement, see paras 6.17, 6.18.

1.4   On 13 November 2001 the Lord Chancellor made the following statement in the House of Lords in relation to the timetable for implementing the Act—

> 'The Act will be fully implemented by January 2005, 11 months before the timetable set out in the Act itself. The publication scheme provisions will be implemented first, on a rolling programme, starting with central government in November 2002. I am today placing a full schedule of organisations and dates of implementation in the Libraries of both Houses. This roll-out will be completed in June 2004, and the individual right of access to information held by all public authorities, including government departments, will be implemented in January 2005'.[1]

---
[1]   HL Debates, 13 November 2001, col 457.

PREPARATION

1.5   Much of the detailed content of the scheme created by FOIA 2000 is to be provided by subordinate legislation and by codes of practice issued under the Act. At present there are two draft codes of practice in existence, one on records management and one on the discharge of functions under the Act.[1] In the absence of this material, what can be said about the operation of the Act remains speculative. Nevertheless, it would be unwise for public authorities to disregard the legislation. In particular, they need to be aware that, when it comes into force, FOIA 2000 will, to some extent, be retrospective in its effect. It will apply to information already in their possession, and not merely to information that comes into their possession after FOIA 2000 comes into force. Public authorities need to bear in mind from now on that they have already received, and are now receiving, information that will in due course become subject to disclosure under FOIA 2000.[2]

---
[1]   At the time of writing, these draft codes are the subject of consultation with the Information Commissioner and the Northern Ireland Minister; see Appendix 2.
[2]   As to the meaning of 'public authority' see paras 3.9–3.15.

1.6   This book is intended to assist in understanding FOIA 2000, and, inter alia, to help public authorities prepare for the time when FOIA 2000 is fully in force. It is also intended to provide guidance to others who may wish to use it once it is fully in force.

1.7 The Act has proved controversial. There has been considerable criticism from those favouring a wide-ranging freedom of information regime, who feel that FOIA 2000 represents a retreat from the government's initial radicalism on this issue.[1] Freedom of information is likely to remain a subject of political controversy for many years. For this reason, we begin with an attempt to put FOIA 2000 in context, looking both at international experience and at the historical background to the Act itself.

---

[1] See for instance the material on the website of the Campaign for Freedom of Information: www.cfoi.org.uk.

INTERNATIONAL EXPERIENCE

1.8 Freedom of information legislation (FOI legislation) is well established in a number of common law and European jurisdictions. For instance, in the United States of America, FOI legislation in relation to federal government was enacted as early as 1966.[1]

---

[1] For a useful summary of the regimes in a number of other jurisdictions, see Table 1 of the consultation document on the draft Bill, (Cm 4355), at pp 13, 14.

1.9 Those drafting FOI legislation face a common set of problems whatever jurisdiction they work in. They need to define the scope of application of the legislation, ie, what information is covered, and in whose hands. They need to provide for an appeal process where disclosure is refused, and to consider whether this should be by internal agency review only, or by appeal to a specially created body, or by appeal to the ordinary courts. They also need to consider what exemptions from disclosure should be given in respect of, for instance, national security. Some examples of how these problems have been dealt with in various jurisdictions are set out below.

United States

1.10 The US legislation covers all agencies in the executive branch of federal government. The legislation covers 'records' (in practice this applies to information in any form). Appeals against non-disclosure are dealt with by internal agency review, with a right of appeal to the courts thereafter. In addition a number of states have their own FOI legislation, of varying scope.

Australia, Canada and New Zealand

1.11 Australia, Canada and New Zealand all enacted FOI legislation in 1982. The Australian legislation gives a right of access to official 'documents' (defined broadly, and including information stored electronically). It covers federal government and many agencies. Appeals against non-disclosure are made to an Ombudsman and an Administrative Appeals Tribunal (which can make binding orders for disclosure), and thereafter to the Federal Court. The Canadian legislation gives a right of access to 'records' (including machine readable records). As with the Australian legislation, it covers federal government and a number of state agencies. Appeals against non-disclosure are made to an Ombudsman (who makes non-binding recommendations) with a further appeal to the Federal Court. The New Zealand legislation covers official information (including information recorded or stored on computers or other devices) and material derived from such information. Appeals against non-disclosure are made to an Ombudsman. Ministers collectively have the right to veto the Ombudsman's recommendation that information be disclosed; this is done by an Order in Council made within 21 days of the recommendation. There is express provision for judicial review of the veto on the ground that it is beyond the powers conferred by the FOI legislation or is otherwise wrong in law.

France

1.12 France enacted FOI legislation in 1978. The legislation gives a right of access to 'administrative documents', including non-personal computerised information. There is a commission for access to administrative documents, and applications are made through this body. Appeals are dealt with through the courts.

The Netherlands

1.13 The Netherlands enacted FOI legislation in 1991. The legislation covers information contained in 'documents', which are widely defined (including non-written material containing data). It covers central and local government, public bodies and statutory organisations. Appeals are dealt with through the courts.

Ireland

1.14 Ireland enacted FOI legislation in 1998. There is a right of access to official information contained in 'records'. There is an extensive definition of information, including records stored mechanically or electronically. Appeals are determined by an Information Commissioner, whose decisions are binding.

1.15 FOI legislation in all of the above jurisdictions includes a range of exemptions. These are usually intended to protect specific interests (eg, national security or the confidentiality of sensitive information). Sometimes the threshold for an exemption to operate is set very low (eg, any possibility of harm to the specified interest will bring the exemption into operation). Sometimes it is set very high (eg, there must be a probability of serious harm for the exemption to take effect).

THE REGIME IN THE UK PRIOR TO FOIA 2000

1.16 On 4 April 1994 the Conservative government introduced a 'Code of Practice on Access to Government Information'.

1.17 The 1994 code of practice was a significant step towards FOI legislation, but there were a number of important limitations to it. Most fundamentally, it did not create an enforceable legal obligation to disclose information. The only sanction for a breach of the code was that the person seeking information could complain to the Parliamentary Ombudsman. There were other important limitations too. The code only applied to government departments and those other bodies that were subject to the Parliamentary Ombudsman's jurisdiction. Complaints could not be made directly to the Parliamentary Ombudsman, but had to be made via a member of Parliament. The code only required the disclosure of information, and not of documents. There were 15 categories of exempt information, some of them extremely broad. A separate 'Code of Practice on Openness in the NHS' came into force on 1 June 1995.

THE WHITE PAPER

1.18 The White Paper published by the Labour government in December 1997[1] was welcomed by campaigners for FOI legislation as a surprisingly radical document.[2] The proposed legislation was to cover the whole of the public sector, together with the privatised utilities and the work of private bodies in relation to functions contracted out to them by the public sector. All information (including unrecorded information) was to be covered, as well as all forms of records (including electronic records). An independent Information Commissioner was to have the power to compel disclosure, and the government was to have no power to veto the

Commissioner's decisions. Importantly, although the White Paper did not set out in full the scope of the proposed exemptions, it did make it clear that, in general, the test for an exemption would be whether the proposed disclosure would cause 'substantial harm' to a specified interest, and not merely whether it would harm that interest.[3]

---

[1]   Cm 3818 (December 1997).
[2]   See eg, 'Unlocking the Truth: the Government's FOI White Paper', by Maurice Frankel of the Campaign for Freedom of Information, Guardian, 16 December 1997.
[3]   Cm 3818, para 3.7.

THE DRAFT BILL

1.19   A consultation document, including the text of a draft Bill, was published in May 1999.[1] A considerable period had elapsed since the White Paper, and many commentators regarded the Bill as a substantial retreat from the radicalism of the earlier proposals. Criticism was focused on the breadth of the exemptions included in the Bill. In particular, for some areas (notably safety investigations and the background to policy decisions by public bodies) blanket exemptions applied without there being any specific requirement to show a risk that disclosure would harm a specific interest.[2] The role for the proposed Information Commissioner was also diminished. Where information was exempt from disclosure, public authorities were to have the power to disclose it, but the Information Commissioner would not be able to compel them to exercise that power. His role would be limited to ensuring only that the public interest in disclosure be considered, and requiring reconsideration of the matter if the public authority had failed to take the public interest into account.[3]

---

[1]   See para 1.2.
[2]   As to the exemptions contained in FOIA 2000, see Ch 4.
[3]   As to the Information Commissioner, see para 3.52 et seq.

THE ACT

1.20   A Bill was finally introduced into the House of Commons in December 1999. The Bill was amended during its passage through Parliament, and in general, the effect of the amendments was to strengthen the legislation. However, overall there is no doubt that much of the initial radicalism of the White Paper has not been carried into effect in the Act.

1.21 In particular, FOIA 2000 incorporates wide-ranging exemptions in relation to the disclosure of information relating to the formation of government policy. Further, the decisions of the Information Commissioner as to whether or not information that allegedly falls within an exemption should be disclosed are, in many cases, subject to being overruled by government.

STRUCTURE OF THE BOOK

1.22 This book, so far as possible, treats FOIA 2000 as if it was already fully in force (while recognising that a number of important elements remain to be provided by subordinate legislation and codes of practice).

1.23 The book is intended to be of assistance both to public authorities faced with the prospect of implementing the legislation, and to those who may wish to use it in order to obtain information from those authorities. Chapter 2 outlines the structure of FOIA 2000, and provides a brief 'user's guide' from the perspective both of public authorities and of applicants for information. Chapters 3–7 contain a commentary on the provisions of FOIA 2000.

2 A brief user's guide to the Act

INTRODUCTION

2.1 The following chapters of this book analyse the Freedom of Information Act 2000 (FOIA 2000) in detail. This chapter is intended to be a brief 'user's guide' to the Act, both for those who wish to make applications for information under the Act, and for public bodies required to consider such applications. Our intention is to answer the main practical questions that may be raised by potential users of the Act.

2.2 We begin with a short summary of the structure of the Act (see paras 2.3–2.13). We go on to consider the Act from the perspective of a person seeking information (see paras 2.14–2.22), and then from the perspective of a public body faced with a request for information (see paras 2.23–2.28).

AN OVERVIEW OF THE ACT

General principle

2.3 The Act imposes a wide general duty on public authorities to disclose information on request, and also imposes a wide range of qualifications to that duty.

2.4 The general principle is stated in FOIA 2000, s 1(1). Where a person makes a request for information to a public authority, the authority has a duty to—

(1) inform the applicant, in writing, whether it holds information of the description specified in the request (s 1(1)(a)) (this duty is referred to in the Act as 'the duty to confirm or deny' (s 1(6));

(2) communicate information (if it does hold information of the requested description) to the applicant (s 1(1)(b)). The Act does not give a convenient label to this duty, but we refer to it as 'the duty to communicate'.

Exemptions — Exemptions

2.5 There are a number of exemptions to the general duty imposed by s 1(1) (see s 2 and ss 21–44). With one exception, these exemptions apply both in relation to the duty to confirm or deny and in relation to the duty to communicate.[1] Some of these exemptions are absolute. Where there is an absolute exemption, the public body is not subject to the particular duty to which the exemption relates. Other exemptions are not absolute, in which case the question is whether the public interest in maintaining the exemption outweighs the public interest in the performance of the duty. If it does, then the public authority is not subject to the particular duty to which the exemption relates.

---

[1] The exception is s 21: exemption for information reasonably accessible otherwise than under FOIA 2000. This exemption applies only to the duty to communicate.

2.6 In addition to the specific exemptions set out in Pt II of the Act, there are two general exemptions contained in ss 12 and 14. Under s 12, a public authority is not obliged to comply with a request for information if the authority estimates that the cost of compliance would exceed the 'appropriate limit' (this is to be prescribed by regulations made by the Secretary of State under s 12(3)).

2.7 Under s 14 of the Act, a public authority is not obliged to comply with a vexatious request, or with repeated identical or substantially similar requests (unless a reasonable interval has elapsed between them). The effect of these provisions is to exclude both the duty to confirm or deny and the duty to communicate.

2.8 The specific exemptions in Pt II (ss 21–44) are considered in more detail in Ch 4.[1] However, a summary is set out in the Table below. It states whether or not the exclusion is absolute and whether it applies in relation to both the duty to confirm or deny and the duty to communicate, or only in relation to one of them.

Nature of exemption	Is it absolute?	Duties excluded
Information accessible to applicant by other means (s 21)	Yes	Duty to communicate
Information intended for future publication (s 22)	No	Both duties
Information from bodies relating to security matters (s 23)	Yes	Both duties
Information required to safeguard national security (s 24)	No	Both duties

Nature of exemption	Is it absolute?	Duties excluded
Information likely to prejudice defence (s 26)	No	Both duties
Information likely to prejudice international relations (s 27)	No	Both duties
Information likely to prejudice relations between UK administrations (s 28)	No	Both duties
Information likely to prejudice economic interests (s 29)	No	Both duties
Information obtained for the purpose of investigations and proceedings conducted by public authorities (s 30)	No	Both duties
Information likely to prejudice law enforcement (s 31)	No	Both duties
Court records (etc) (s 32)	Yes	Both duties
Information related to public sector audit functions (s 33)	No	Both duties
Information subject to Parliamentary privilege (s 34)	Yes	Both duties
Information relating to the formulation of government policy (s 35)	No	Both duties
Information likely to prejudice the effective conduct of public affairs (s 36)	Yes (in part)	Both duties
Communications with the Royal Family (etc) (s 37)	No	Both duties
Information likely to endanger the health or safety of any individual (s 38)	No	Both duties
Information covered by regulations made under s 74 (implementing the Aarhus Convention relating to environmental information) (s 39)	No	Both duties
Certain personal data of which the applicant is the data subject (s 40)	Yes (in part)	Both duties
Information the disclosure of which would be an actionable breach of confidence (s 41)	Yes	Both duties
Information subject to legal professional privilege (s 42)	No	Both duties
Information that constitutes a trade secret (s 43)	No	Both duties
Information the disclosure of which is prohibited (otherwise than under FOIA 2000) (s 44)	Yes	Both duties

See paras 4.15–4.90

The Commissioner and the Tribunal

2.9 Under FOIA 2000, the Data Protection Commissioner is to be known as the Information Commissioner, and the Data Protection Tribunal is to be known as the Information Tribunal (see s 18). These are referred to in FOIA 2000 as the Commissioner and the Tribunal respectively. A number of functions are conferred on the Commissioner, the Tribunal, the Secretary of State, and the Lord Chancellor.

Code of Practice

2.10 The Secretary of State is to issue a code of practice providing guidance to public authorities on the discharge of their functions under FOIA 2000, Pt I (s 45(1)). The Lord Chancellor is to issue a code of practice providing guidance to public authorities on desirable practice in relation to the keeping, management and destruction of records (s 46(1)). Draft codes of practice under both sections have now been issued.[1] The Commissioner has a general duty to promote the following of good practice under the Act (s 47) and a power to give specific recommendations to particular public authorities that appear to him not to be complying with the codes issued under ss 45 and 46 (see s 48).

---

[1] See Appendix 2. Responsibility for freedom of information and data protection was transferred from the Home Office to the Lord Chancellor's Department (LCD); see the Transfer of Functions (Miscellaneous) Order 2001, SI 2001/3500. The Freedom of Information and Data Protection Division at LCD is part of the Department's Policy Group. Hence, the Lord Chancellor's Department is actually responsible for both draft codes of practice.

Enforcement and appeals

2.11 Parts IV (ss 50–56) and V (ss 57–61) of the Act deal respectively with enforcement and rights of appeal. If an applicant for information wishes to challenge a public authority's failure to disclose, the first step is to apply to the Commissioner for a decision as to whether the public authority has complied with the requirements of Pt I of the Act (see s 50). A person applying to the Commissioner for such a decision is referred to in the Act as 'the complainant' (s 50(1)). The Commissioner must either notify the complainant that he has made no decision, together with his grounds for making no decision, or serve a decision notice on the complainant and the public authority (s 50(3)). Where the Commissioner is satisfied that a public authority has failed to comply with any of the requirements of Pt I of the Act, he may serve an enforcement notice setting out the steps that he requires the authority to take in order to comply with the Act (s 52). The Commissioner can also serve a notice (an information notice) under s 51 requiring the public authority to provide him with information relevant to his various enforcement functions under the Act. If a public authority has failed to comply with so much of a decision notice as requires steps to be taken, an information notice, or an enforcement notice, the Commissioner can certify to the court that there has been such a failure. In those circumstances the court (after hearing evidence and submissions for the public authority) can deal with the authority as if it had committed a contempt of court (s 54).

2.12   Both the complainant and the public authority may appeal to the Tribunal against a decision notice of the Commissioner (s 57(1)) and the public authority may appeal against an enforcement notice (s 57(2)). There is a further right of appeal from the Tribunal, on a point of law, to the High Court of Justice in England, the Court of Session in Scotland, or the High Court of Justice in Northern Ireland (s 59).

Records

2.13   Part VI (ss 62–67) of the Act deals with historical records and records in the Public Record Office or Public Record Office of Northern Ireland. Part VII (ss 68–73) of the Act amends the Data Protection Act 1998. Part VIII (ss 74–88) deals with various miscellaneous and supplemental matters.

MAKING A REQUEST FOR INFORMATION

2.14   Some practical questions that may be asked by a person requesting information are dealt with in paras 2.15–2.22.

How do I request information under FOIA 2000?

2.15   The first step is to identify the public authority that you think holds the information that you are seeking. You should then direct your request to that authority. The request must be in writing, must include your name and an address for correspondence, and must describe the information requested (s 8(1)). It is not necessary to say that you are making a request under FOIA 2000, but it would be advisable to include this. You should also consider specifying in your request the format in which you would like the information to be provided to you. You should refer to FOIA 2000, s 11, under which you can express a preference for one or more out of three specified modes of communication.[1]

---

[1]   See para 2.20.

Can I send a request by e-mail?

2.16 Yes. Under the Act it is sufficient if the request is electronically transmitted, is received in legible form, and is capable of being used for subsequent reference (s 8(2)).

How much detail do I need to give about what I am asking for?

2.17 You should give as much detail as you can. If the public authority is not clear as to what you are asking for, it can ask you for further information in order to identify and locate what it is you are requesting. The public authority is not obliged to disclose information to you until you have complied with such a request (s 1(3)). Therefore, if your request lacks detail there may be a delay in dealing with it.

What if I need help in formulating my request?

2.18 Public bodies are under a duty to provide reasonable advice and assistance to persons applying, or proposing to apply, for information (s 16). The code of practice to be issued by the Secretary of State under s 45 will provide further guidance about what this requires in practice.

How soon will I be given the information requested?

2.19 In general, your request must be answered by not later than the twentieth working day following your application (s 10(1)). However, the Secretary of State has power by regulations to extend this period to a date not later than the sixtieth working day (s 10(4)). A public authority may be entitled to take longer to consider your request in cases where it needs time to decide whether or not one of the non-absolute exemptions applies.

What format will be used to communicate the information to me?

2.20 The first point to note is that FOIA 2000 confers a right to receive *information* and not a right to receive *documents*. However, FOIA 2000, s 11(1) provides that you may express a preference for one or more of the following options—
  (a) the provision of a copy of the information in permanent form or another form acceptable to you;
  (b) the provision of a reasonable opportunity to inspect a record containing the information; and
  (c) the provision to you of a digest or summary of the information in permanent form or another form acceptable to you.

The public authority has to comply with your preference as far as is reasonably practicable. Note that you may choose *one or more* of the specified options, therefore you could ask both to receive information in permanent form and to inspect the relevant records yourself.

Will I have to pay for the information?

2.21   A public authority may serve a fees notice on you (s 9(1)). The level of fees is to be determined by regulations to be made by the Secretary of State (s 9(3)). Where a fees notice has been given to you, the public authority is not obliged to provide information to you unless you pay the fee within three months beginning on the day on which the fees notice is given to you (s 9(2)). Assuming that you pay the fee, the authority still has 20 working days in which to answer your request, but in calculating that period of 20 days, the working days during the period beginning when the fees notice was served on you and ending when you paid the fee are disregarded (s 10(2)).

What can I do if the information requested is refused?

2.22   Your first step is to apply to the Commissioner for a decision as to whether or not the public authority has complied with the Act (s 50(1)). There is no specific time limit for making this application, but you should act as soon as possible, as the Commissioner has power to refuse to consider your application if he thinks that you have been guilty of undue delay (s 50(2)(b)). If the Commissioner issues a decision notice, you can appeal against it to the Tribunal (s 57(1)). You may be able to appeal to the court against a decision of the Tribunal, if a point of law is involved (s 59).[1]

---

[1]   See paras 2.11, 2.12.

COMPLYING WITH THE ACT

Public authorities

2.23   Paragraphs 2.24–2.28 discuss FOIA 2000 from the perspective of a public authority that is responding to an application for information.

Must we comply with a request for information?

2.24   The general principle is that you must comply both with the duty to communicate and with the duty to disclose. This is subject to the detailed exemptions in Pt II (ss 21–44) of the Act. Where the Pt II exemptions do not apply, the other circumstances in which you need not comply are as follows—

(1) Where you reasonably require further information from the applicant in order to comply with his request, and that further information has not been provided (s 1(3)).

(2) Where you have served a fees notice and the applicant has not paid the fee within three months (s 9(2)).

(3) Where the cost of compliance would exceed the appropriate limit as defined in regulations to be made by the Secretary of State (note however, that this does not exempt a public authority from compliance with the duty to confirm or deny under s 1, unless the cost of compliance with that duty alone would exceed the appropriate limit) (s 12).

(4) Where the request is vexatious (s 14(1)).

(5) Where the request is identical or substantially similar to a previous request by the same person and the previous request has been complied with (unless a reasonable time has elapsed since the previous request was made) (s 14(2)).

Who decides whether or not one of the exemptions applies?

2.25 In the first instance, you do. This means that where you are not considering one of the absolute exemptions you will need to carry out the balancing exercise required by s 2(1)(b) and/or s 2(2)(b). Therefore, you will need to consider whether the public interest in maintaining the exclusion outweighs the public interest in disclosure. However, if you decide to rely on the exemption, your decision may be challenged by a complaint to the Commissioner.

What if we need more time in order to decide whether an exemption applies?

2.26 The general rule is that you must provide the information requested not later than the twentieth working day following the date of receipt of the request. However, if you need more time in order to consider whether or not an exemption applies (other than an absolute exemption) you are entitled to such additional time as is reasonable in the circumstances (s 10). You must, however, give the applicant a notice that you are still considering whether or not an exemption applies, and that notice must be served not later than the twentieth working day following the date of receipt of the applicant's request.

Do we have to comply with the decisions of the Commissioner?

2.27 If the Commissioner decides that you have failed to comply with your duty under FOIA 2000, s 1(1) he may issue a decision notice or an enforcement notice to that effect. If you fail to comply with such a notice, your failure may be certified to the court, and the court may deal with it as if you had committed a contempt of court (s 54).

2.28 There are, however, two ways in which a decision notice or enforcement notice may be rendered ineffective. First, you may appeal to the Tribunal (s 57). In that case, until the appeal has been determined or withdrawn, no step which is affected by the appeal need be taken. Secondly, where a decision or enforcement notice is served on a government department or on certain other bodies, the 'accountable person' (in relation to most public bodies this will be a Cabinet Minister) may certify that there was no failure to comply with the duty to confirm or deny or the duty to disclose (s 53). The effect of the certificate is that the decision or enforcement notice to which it relates ceases to have effect. This power only relates to cases falling within one of the exemptions in Pt II of the Act.

3 The general right of access to information held by public authorities

INTRODUCTION

3.1 This chapter focuses on the provisions of FOIA 2000, Pt I (ss 1–20) that establish a general right of access to information held by public authorities. As explained in Ch 2, the Act establishes a general right and then sets out a number of specific exemptions.[1] Most of the exemptions are set out in Pt II (ss 21–44).[2]

---

[1] See para 2.3 et seq.
[2] See further Ch 4.

SECTION 1(1): THE GENERAL RIGHT

Request for information ✓

3.2 Section 1(1) creates what is at first sight a wide general right of access to information held by public authorities. It provides that—

'Any person making a request for information to a public authority is entitled—
(a) to be informed in writing by the public authority whether it holds information of the description specified in the request, and
(b) if that is the case, to have that information communicated to him.'

3.3 Section 1(1) has effect subject to the provisions of ss 1(3)–(6), 2, 9, 12 and 14 (see s 1(2)). Section 2 (relating to exemptions) is considered in detail in Ch 4. The other provisions mentioned in s 1(2) are considered further below.[1]

---

[1] See paras 3.28–3.42.

duty to confirm or deny. Duty to communicate

3.4   Section 1(1) creates two separate rights, and therefore imposes two separate duties on public authorities. The duty under s 1(1)(a) is referred to in the Act as 'the duty to confirm or deny' (s 1(6)). Unhelpfully, the Act does not use a similar convenient label for the duty under s 1(1)(b). We refer to this duty as 'the duty to communicate'. Although there are two separate duties, compliance with the duty to communicate will also satisfy the duty to confirm or deny (s 1(5)).

3.5   Section 1(1) raises a number of questions. What is 'information'? What is a 'public authority'? In what form must a request be made and answered? Within how long must it be answered? What are the qualifications on the general right of access under s 1(1)? These questions are discussed at paras 3.6–3.42.

WHAT IS 'INFORMATION'?

3.6   The concept of 'information' is of central importance to FOIA 2000. There is a definition in s 84—

> '"information" (subject to sections 51(8) and 75(2)) means information recorded in any form.'

Therefore, for example, information recorded in a computer database would fall within the duty of disclosure in s 1(1). On the other hand, information that is known to an individual within a public authority but which is not recorded in any form would appear to fall outside s 1(1). So if a public sector employee is told something but makes no record of what he has been told then there is no duty of disclosure in relation to this item of information. It remains to be seen whether an unintended effect of the Act will be a greater reliance by public authorities on unrecorded information.

3.7   Section 1(4) imposes an important limitation on s 1(1). The duty to confirm or deny and the duty to communicate will operate in relation to the information held 'at the time when the request is received'. The only exception to this is that account may be taken of any amendment or deletion made between the time when the request is received and the time when the information is to be communicated. Hence, the Act does not confer a right to be told whether the public authority has *in the past* held information of a particular kind. This may create difficulties for an individual seeking to find out whether particular records existed previously which have since been destroyed.

3.8   The solution to this problem may be to request information held now as to whether records were destroyed at some point in the past, and as to the nature of the records that were destroyed. However, this will not

18

help the applicant in cases where the destruction of records was itself unrecorded. Further, although s 77 creates an offence of altering records with intent to prevent disclosure, the offence is not committed unless the alteration took place after a request for the information was received. There seems to be nothing in the Act that will effectively prevent public authorities from 'weeding' records in advance of any request under FOIA 2000. It remains to be seen whether the code of practice to be issued by the Lord Chancellor under s 46 of the Act (dealing, among other matters, with the destruction of records) will contain provisions to address this point.

WHAT IS A PUBLIC AUTHORITY?

3.9   Sections 3–7 of, and Sch 1 to, the Act contain elaborate provisions defining public authority for the purposes of the Act.

3.10   In general, four kinds of public authority are recognised—
    (1) bodies,
    (2) persons,
    (3) holders of an office,
    (4) publicly-owned companies.

In relation to the first three, FOIA 2000 does not provide a general definition, but instead relies mainly on a long list set out in Sch 1. The Act does, however, provide a general definition of a publicly-owned company.[1]

---
[1]   See para 3.14.

3.11   A body, person, or office-holder will be a public authority if listed in Sch 1 to the Act (see s 3(1)(a)(i)). Schedule 1 includes a number of obvious examples of public authorities: any government department, the House of Commons, the House of Lords, the Northern Ireland Assembly, the National Assembly for Wales, the armed forces of the Crown,[1] a local authority within the meaning of the Local Government Act 1972, and the Greater London Authority. A wide range of NHS bodies (see Sch 1, Pt III), educational institutions (Sch 1, Pt IV), and police bodies (Sch 1, Pt V) are also included. Schedule 1, Pt VI contains a long list of other bodies which are public authorities for the purposes of the Act. They range from the Advisory Board on the Registration of Homeopathic Products, via the Indian Family Pensions Funds Body of Commissioners, to the Zoos Forum. Part VII contains a similar list for Northern Ireland.

₁   But not the special forces, or any unit or part of a unit which is for the time being required by the Secretary of State to assist the Government Communications Headquarters in the exercise of its functions.

3.12   Section 4 allows the Secretary of State to amend Sch 1 by order so as to add bodies or office-holders to the Schedule. Two conditions must be satisfied. First, the body or office must be established under Royal prerogative, primary or subordinate legislation, or in any other way by a Minister of the Crown acting in that capacity, by a government department, or by the National Assembly for Wales (s 4(2)). The second condition is that (in the case of a body) the body must be wholly or partly constituted by appointment made by the Crown, a Minister of the Crown, a government department or the National Assembly for Wales; and (in the case of an office) appointments to the office must be made by the Crown, a Minister of the Crown, a government department or the National Assembly for Wales (s 4(3)). The Secretary of State may also remove bodies or offices from the list in Sch 1 should they cease to exist or cease to satisfy the conditions set out in s 4(2) and (3) (see s 4(4)).

3.13   Under s 5, a person who is not listed in Sch 1 and who is not capable of being added to the Schedule under s 4, may be designated a public authority for the purposes of the Act by an order made by the Secretary of State. A person may be so designated if he appears to the Secretary of State to exercise functions of a public nature (s 5(1)(a)) or if he is providing, under a contract made with a public authority, any service whose provision is a function of that authority (s 5(1)(b)). It follows that a private sector company providing services under contract with a public authority may be designated as a public authority.

3.14   Section 6 sets out a definition of a publicly-owned company. A company is publicly-owned if it is wholly owned by the Crown (s 6(1)(a)), or if it is wholly owned by any public authority listed in Sch 1 other than a government department or an authority that is listed only in relation to particular information (s 6(1)(b)).

3.15   Section 7 of the Act recognises that some public authorities are listed in Sch 1 only in relation to information of a specified description. In the case of such authorities, Pts I to V of the Act do not apply to any other information held by the authority. Likewise, an order under s 4(1) (adding a public authority to Sch 1) may list that public authority only in relation to information of a specified description. An order under s 5(1)(a) must specify the functions of the public body in respect of which the designation is to have effect (see s 7(5)); and an order under s 5(1)(b) must specify the services provided under contract in respect of which the designation is to take effect (see s 7(6)).

WHAT FORM SHOULD A REQUEST TAKE?

3.16 Section 8 specifies the form that a request for information must take. The formal requirements are limited. The request must be in writing, it must state the name of the applicant and give an address for correspondence, and it must describe the information requested (s 8(1)). Although there is a requirement that the request should be in writing, it appears that e-mail will suffice. Under s 8(2), a request is to be treated as made in writing where the text of it is transmitted by electronic means, is received in legible form and is capable of being used for subsequent reference.

3.17 There is no specific requirement that the request should state that it is made under FOIA 2000. It is, however, suggested that it would be advisable for applicants to include this in their written requests, especially while the Act remains comparatively unfamiliar.

3.18 There is no specific provision in the Act about how much detail must be given by an applicant concerning the nature of the information that he is seeking. However, s 1(3) of the Act makes provision for a situation in which a public authority reasonably requires further information from an applicant in order to identify and locate the information requested. Where the authority informs the applicant of that requirement, it is not obliged to comply with the duty to confirm or deny, or the duty to communicate, unless it is supplied with that further information. It follows that an applicant is well advised to identify with as much precision as possible the information sought. Failure to do so may permit a public authority to delay dealing with the request.

3.19 A public authority is under a general duty to provide reasonable advice and assistance to persons who propose to make, or have made, requests for information to it (s 16(1)). Section 16(2) envisages that the code of practice to be issued by the Secretary of State under s 45 of the Act will provide guidance as to what is required under s 16(1). Section 16(2) states that any public authority which conforms with that code in relation to the provision of advice or assistance is to be taken to have complied with its duty under s 16(1).

3.20 It is suggested that there is some risk of an impasse being reached between a public authority and an applicant. The authority may contend that it needs more information in order to answer the applicant's request, while the applicant argues that he has given as much information as he can, and that any further relevant information is actually in the hands of the public authority. It is to be hoped that s 16 will prevent this sort of difficulty from arising.

WHEN, AND HOW, MUST A REQUEST BE ANSWERED?

Time limit for compliance with request

3.21   Section 10(1) sets out a general time limit. A public authority must comply promptly with its duty to confirm or deny and its duty to communicate. It must in any event comply with those duties not later than the twentieth working day following the date of receipt of the applicant's request. However, there are a number of qualifications to this time limit.

3.22   One qualification applies in cases where the public authority gives the applicant a fees notice under s 9 of the Act.[1] In that case, the working days beginning with the day on which the fees notice is given to the applicant and ending with the day on which the fee is received by the authority are to be disregarded in calculating the 20-day limit (see s 10(2)).

---

[1]   See paras 3.28–3.32.

3.23   A further qualification is set out in s 10(3). This provision applies in cases where one of the non-absolute exemptions applies in relation to either the duty to confirm or deny, or the duty to communicate. In other words, the provision relates to cases in which it is necessary (under s 2(1)(b) or 2(2)(b)) to consider whether the public interest in maintaining the relevant exemption outweighs the public interest in disclosure. In these cases, the public authority need not comply with its duties under s 1(1) of the Act until such time as is reasonable in the circumstances. Clearly, the purpose of the provision is to allow more time to public authorities in order to enable them to carry out the rather difficult balancing exercise required by s 2(1)(b) and s 2(2)(b). However, in such a case the public authority must, within the time limit for complying with s 1(1), serve a notice stating that an exemption applies, identifying the exemption, and giving an estimate of the date by which the authority expects that a decision will have been reached on the application of the exemption (s 17(2)).

3.24   As already discussed, where a public authority reasonably requires further information before answering a request, and has informed the applicant of that requirement, the authority is not obliged to answer the request until the further information has been provided.[1] In such a case, time under s 10(1) does not begin to run until the authority has received the further information (s 10(6)(b)).

---

[1]   See para 3.18.

3.25   Section 10(4) and (5) confer powers on the Secretary of State to make regulations to extend the basic time limit in s 10(1). Such regulations may provide that s 10(1) and (2) are to have effect as if any reference to the twentieth working day following the date of receipt were a reference to some other day, not later than the sixtieth working day following the date of receipt. Such regulations may prescribe different days in relation to different cases and may confer a discretion on the Commissioner.

Method of response

3.26   As to the means by which any response by a public authority is to be made, the public authority may in general comply by communicating information by any means which are reasonable in the circumstances (s 11(4)). However, when he makes his request for information the applicant is entitled to express a preference for communication by one or more of three specified means (s 11(1)). Note that the applicant may chose one *or more* of the means; he does not have to choose between them. Section 11(1) provides that the three specified means are—
  '(a)   the provision to the applicant of a copy of the information in permanent form or another form acceptable to the applicant,
  (b)   the provision to the applicant of a reasonable opportunity to inspect a record containing the information, and
  (c)   the provision to the applicant of a digest or summary of the information in permanent form or in another form acceptable to the applicant'.

3.27   Where the applicant expresses a preference for one or more of the specified means, the public authority must give effect to it so far as reasonably practicable (s 11(1)). Where the public authority determines that it is not reasonably practicable to comply with the preferred means of communication it must notify the applicant of the reasons for its determination (s 11(3)). The question of reasonable practicability is to by determined having regard to all the circumstances, including cost (s 11(2)).

FEES AND COSTS OF COMPLIANCE

3.28   Part I of the Act deals with the question of cost in two main ways—
  (1)   It provides for a general power to charge fees.
  (2)   It specifically provides as to how a public authority is to deal with certain particularly costly requests.

In relation to these the Act only sets out a framework, leaving the details to be completed by regulations.

Fees

3.29   Section 9(1) provides that a public authority to whom a request for information is made may give the applicant a fees notice specifying the fee to be charged by the authority for complying with its s 1(1) duty to confirm or deny and its duty to communicate. The amount of any fee is to be determined in accordance with regulations to be made by the Secretary of State (s 9(3)).

3.30   Any fees notice must be given to the applicant within the period for complying with s 1(1) (see s 9(1)). It follows that, unless one of the exceptions to s 10(1) applies, the fees notice must be given to the applicant not later than the twentieth working day following the date of receipt of his request.

3.31   Where a fees notice is given to the applicant, the effect of s 10(2) (as discussed earlier)[1] is that the time between the giving of the notice and the receipt of the fee does not count in determining what is the twentieth working day following the date of receipt of the applicant's request. This means that time for compliance with the public authority's duty does not run during the period when a fees notice remains unpaid.

---

[1]   See para 3.22.

3.32   If a fees notice is given to an applicant a week after he makes his request, and he pays the fee two months later, then the authority must comply with s 1(1) of the Act. If a fees notice is given to an applicant a month after he makes his request, this will usually mean that the fees notice is of no effect because it was given outside the statutory time limit for compliance with the Act (s 9(1)). If a fees notice is given to the applicant within the statutory time limit for compliance and the applicant does not pay the fee until after the period of three months has expired, then the public authority is under no duty to comply with the s 1(1) duty (see s 9(2)). Presumably in such a case, if the public authority proposed not to comply with s 1(1), it would be obliged to return to the applicant the fee that he had paid.

Exceeding appropriate limit

3.33   There are also special provisions in ss 12 and 13 covering particularly expensive requests. Under s 12(1), a public authority is under no duty to comply with a request for information if it estimates that the cost of compliance would exceed the 'appropriate limit'. This limit is to be prescribed by regulations and 'different amounts may be prescribed in relation to different cases' (s 12(3)). An authority is permitted to charge a fee for communicating information where the cost of compliance exceeds the appropriate limit (see s 13). The level of fee that may be charged is to be set by regulations (s 13(1), (2)).

3.34 The combined effect of ss 12 and 13 therefore, is that where a public authority estimates that the cost of complying with a request would exceed the appropriate limit, the authority is not obliged to comply with the request. It may choose to comply with it, and may then charge a fee under s 13. However, it is under no duty to comply, even if the applicant is willing to pay such fee as may be chargeable under s 13.

3.35 This raises the question as to whether the applicant can circumvent the effect of s 12 by making a number of different requests, none of which, taken alone, is likely to exceed the appropriate limit? Section 12(4) is intended to prevent this. It provides that regulations may prescribe circumstances in which a number of requests made by one person, or by different persons who appear to be 'acting in concert or pursuing a campaign', are to be considered together for costs purposes. Where requests are considered together, the estimated cost of complying with any of them is to be taken to be the estimated total cost of complying with them all. It is reasonably clear how this provision would operate in relation to *simultaneous* requests. What is not clear is how it would deal with *consecutive* requests. We return to this point in para 3.40.

VEXATIOUS AND REPEATED REQUESTS

3.36 Section 14 is intended to confer some protection on public authorities in dealing with vexatious and repeated requests. This is not intended to include otherwise valid requests in which the applicant happens to take an opportunity to vent his frustration.[1]

---
1 Explanatory notes to Freedom of Information Act 2000, para 59.

3.37 Under s 14(1), a public authority is not obliged to comply with a request for information if the request is vexatious. There is no further definition in the Act of what is meant by 'vexatious' (see paras 3.39–3.42).

3.38 Under s 14(2), a public authority is not obliged to comply with a request that is identical or substantially similar to a previous request made by the same applicant, unless a reasonable period of time has elapsed between the two requests.

3.39   Section 14(2) does not deal with a situation in which different persons successively make identical or very similar requests within a short period of time. It is suggested however that if the requests were made by individuals acting in concert,[1] then the second and any subsequent requests might well be treated as vexatious under s 14(1).

---

[1]   See para 3.35.

3.40   Section 14(2) also fails to deal with a situation in which the same person successively makes a number of different requests relating to the same subject matter. This might be done in an attempt to escape the effect of s 12(1) (ie, in order to ensure that the cost of complying with any individual request did not exceed the appropriate limit). The tactic would fall outside s 14(2) as the requests would not be identical or substantially similar. Nor is it easy to see how s 12(4) could apply. If each successive request was made only after the previous request had been met, then it is difficult to see how the public authority could aggregate the cost of complying with all of the requests in the manner envisaged by s 12(4).

3.41   Thus, it may be that an individual who wants a great deal of information about a specific subject, and who is concerned that the cost of compliance would exceed the appropriate limit under s 12(1), would be advised to break down his request into a number of separate requests and to make those requests consecutively rather than simultaneously.

3.42   It could be argued that where an individual adopts this approach then the later requests would risk being treated as vexatious and a public authority could refuse to comply with a request for information under s 14(1). If, however, the applicant was acting for a proper purpose, and the requests were reasonably related to that purpose, it is difficult to see how they could be regarded as vexatious.

REFUSAL OF REQUEST

3.43   FOIA 2000 requires a public authority to grant a request for information (ie, it must comply with both the duty to confirm or deny and the duty to communicate) unless there is something in the circumstances of the particular case that exempts it from so doing. This chapter has considered the various provisions in Pt I of the Act that are capable of exempting a public authority from the duty to comply. Chapter 4 will consider the exemptions set out in Pt II of the Act.

3.44   Section 17 of the Act sets out what a public authority must do to notify an applicant that it proposes to refuse his request, whether in reliance on Pt I or on Pt II of the Act.

3.45 Under s 17(1) a public authority which is to any extent relying on a claim that any of the exemptions in Pt II are relevant to the request must give notice to the applicant within the time for complying with s 1(1). The notice must state that fact, specify the exemption in question, and state (if it would not otherwise be apparent) why the exemption applies.

3.46 At first sight the wording of s 17(1) is curious: why doesn't it simply cover any case where a public authority is 'relying' on one of the exemptions, rather than referring to a case where the public authority is 'relying on a claim' that one of the exemptions 'is relevant'? The answer is that the provision is intended to cover three situations—
   (1)   Where the public authority is relying on one of the absolute exemptions.
   (2)   Where the public authority is relying on a non-absolute exemption, but has reached the conclusion that the public interest in maintaining the exemption outweighs the public interest in disclosure.
   (3)   Where the public authority is relying on a non-absolute exemption and has not yet been able to decide whether the public interest in maintaining the exemption outweighs the public interest in disclosure.

In any of these three cases, the public authority must give notice under s 17(1) within the time for compliance with its duty under s 1(1). Therefore, notice under s 17(1) must be given no later than the twentieth working day following the date of receipt of the request (see s 10(1)), unless any of the other provisions of the Act operate so as to extend that period.

3.47 Section 17(2) relates specifically to the case in which a public authority has taken the view that one of the non-absolute exemptions in Pt II applies, but has not yet determined whether or not the public interest in maintaining the exemption outweighs the public interest in disclosure. In such a case, the notice served under s 17(1) must indicate that this issue has not yet been decided, and must give an estimate of the date by which the authority expects that such a decision will have been reached. The authority will be under a duty to reach its decision within a reasonable time (s 10(3)).

3.48 Section 17(3) applies where the public authority has determined that one of the non-absolute exemptions in Pt II applies so as to prevent its duty under s 1(1) from arising. Therefore, it applies in a case where the authority has decided that the public interest in maintaining the exemption in question outweighs the public interest in disclosure. In such a case, the public authority must give its reasons for reaching that conclusion. Those reasons must either be given in the s 17(1) notice itself or in a separate notice to be given within such time as is reasonable in the circumstances.

3.49 Section 17 therefore envisages the following sequence of events in cases where a non-absolute exemption is relevant to a request under the Act—

— A public authority receives a request for information.

— It identifies that one of the non-absolute exemptions in Pt II applies, but it needs time to carry out the statutory balancing exercise between the public interest in maintaining the exemption and the public interest in disclosure.

— The authority will serve a notice under s 17(1), within the time limit specified in s 10(1) (unless that time limit is extended under any of the other provisions of the Act).

— The notice will identify the relevant exemption, will say why that exemption is relevant, and will say when the authority expects to be able to make a decision as to whether or not the exemption applies so as to bar the duty to disclose.

— Subsequently, but within a reasonable time, the public authority will either answer the request (if it concludes that the balance is in favour of the public interest in disclosure) or refuse the request (if it concludes that the balance is in favour of maintaining the exemption).

— If the authority refuses the request it will serve a notice to that effect, giving reasons for its decision, under s 17(1) and/or s 17(3).

3.50 Section 17 imposes a duty on the public authority to explain why the exemption relied upon applies (s 17(1)(c)) and why the public interest in maintaining a non-absolute exemption outweighs the interest in disclosure (s 17(3)). These duties do not arise if, or to the extent that, compliance would involve the disclosure of exempt information (s 17(4)).

3.51 Where a public authority relies, instead of on one of the Pt II exemptions, on a claim that s 12 or s 14 applies, it must serve notice to that effect (s 17(5)). The time limit is the same as for the service of notice under s 17(1) (that is to say, the s 10(1) time limit of no later than the twentieth working day following the date of receipt, unless that time limit is extended by one of the other provisions in the Act).

INFORMATION COMMISSIONER AND INFORMATION TRIBUNAL

3.52 FOIA 2000 makes use of some of the administrative machinery already established under the Data Protection Act 1998. The Data Protection Commissioner and the Data Protection Tribunal are to be known as the Information Commissioner and the Information Tribunal respectively, and are referred to in the Act as the Commissioner and the Tribunal (see s 18).

3.53 The Commissioner and the Tribunal are to carry out three main functions—

(1) to help set standards of good practice,
(2) to provide an appeal mechanism,
(3) to enforce the Act.

Most of these functions are dealt with in detail in Ch 5. Paragraphs 3.54–3.56 of this chapter deal with one aspect of the Commissioner's work, in relation to model publication schemes.

PUBLICATION SCHEMES

3.54 Every public authority will be under a duty to adopt and maintain a publication scheme relating to the publication of information by that authority. Publication schemes must be approved by the Commissioner. The duty to maintain such a scheme is imposed by s 19(1). Section 19(2)–(7) sets out the requirements with which a scheme must comply. On 13 November 2001 the Lord Chancellor stated that the publication scheme provisions would be implemented on a rolling programme, starting with central government in November 2002. This roll-out would be completed in June 2004.[1]

[1] See para 1.4.

3.55 The purpose of a publication scheme, it appears, is not to deal with the way in which an authority is to respond to specific requests for information under FOIA 2000. Rather, the purpose of the scheme is to set out the classes of information which the authority intends to publish and the manner in which it intends to publish them (including whether it intends to make information available free of charge or for payment) (see s 19(2)). This means that the Act imposes a duty on public authorities to take active steps to put information into the public domain.

3.56 The preparation of a publication scheme is likely to be burdensome for some authorities (especially the smaller ones) and they are likely to be assisted if the Commissioner exercises his power under s 20 of the Act to approve model publication schemes in relation to particular classes of public authority. Where an authority adopts such a scheme, providing that the scheme adopted remains in force and relates to the appropriate class of public authority, no further approval from the Commissioner is required (s 20(2)). Where the authority adopts a model scheme with modifications, the Commissioner's approval is required, but only in relation to the modifications (s 20(2)).

SPECIAL PROVISIONS RELATING TO PUBLIC RECORDS OFFICE

3.57   Section 15 of the Act makes special provision in relation to material that has been transferred to the Public Record Office, to another place of deposit appointed by the Lord Chancellor under the Public Records Act 1958, or to the Public Record Office of Northern Ireland. Such material is referred to in the section as a 'transferred public record' (s 15(4)).

3.58   Section 15 is intended to govern a situation where a public authority receives a request for information that is both contained in a transferred public record, and is subject to one of the non-absolute exemptions in Pt II of the Act. The public authority receiving the request must inform the 'responsible authority' of the request. The responsible authority will be determined under the provisions of s 15(5), and depending on the circumstances, it will be either a Minister of the Crown, a Northern Ireland Minister, or the person who appears to the Lord Chancellor or the appropriate Northern Ireland Minister to be primarily concerned. That authority will make the decision as to whether or not the public interest in maintaining the relevant non-absolute exemption outweighs the public interest in disclosure (see s 15(3) as read with s 66(3), (4)). The responsible authority will then inform the appropriate records authority (ie, the Public Records Office or other authority actually holding the record) of its determination.

3.59   The intention is that requests for access to material held in the Public Record Office (and in certain other similar places of statutory deposit) that raise issues relating to the application of the non-absolute exemptions set out in Pt II of the Act, are to be determined by the public authority most closely connected with the subject-matter of the record. They are not to be determined by the public authority that happens to receive the request, or by the records authority that holds the material.

4 Categories of exempt information under FOIA 2000

INTRODUCTION

4.1 As explained in Chs 2 and 3, FOIA 2000 creates a general right of access to information held by public authorities (as set out in s 1(1)) together with a series of exceptions to that right.

4.2 Part I (ss 1–20) of the Act creates a number of exceptions or qualifications to the general right conferred by s 1(1). These apply where—
  — the request for information is lacking in particularity (s 1(3)),
  — a fees notice has been served and the fee has not been paid (s 9),
  — the request would be excessively expensive to comply with (s 12), or
  — the request is vexatious or repeats an earlier request (s 14).[1]

---

[1] See paras 3.18, 3.28–3.42.

4.3 However, the most important exceptions to this general right are set out in FOIA 2000, Pt II (ss 21–44). Part II creates a series of specific exemptions that apply to particular subject matter. The most important factor governing whether or not a request for information is likely to be met, therefore, is not the nature of the applicant, nor the nature of the public authority from which the information is sought, but the type of information that is sought in the request.

GENERAL PRINCIPLES: FOIA 2000, PT II

4.4 In order to understand how FOIA 2000, Pt II is intended to work, it is necessary to read it in conjunction with s 2.

4.5 The first point to understand is that, although s 1(1) creates two distinct duties (the duty to confirm or deny, and what we have called the duty to communicate) the provisions in Pt II almost all confer exemption in relation to both duties. The only exception is s 21 (relating to information that is readily accessible to the applicant by other means), which applies only in relation to the duty to communicate.[1]

[1]   See paras 2.5, 2.8.

4.6   The provisions of Pt II deal separately with the duty to confirm or deny and the duty to communicate. As we shall see when we consider the individual exemptions,1 there may be important differences between the scope of the exemption in relation to the duty to confirm or deny and in relation to the duty to communicate.

[1]   See paras 4.15 et seq.

4.7   It is important to remember that although we use the term 'the duty to communicate' as a convenient label for the duty created by s 1(1)(b), this is not a term that is used in the Act. The drafting of the various exemptions in FOIA 2000, Pt II provides that certain information is 'exempt information' for the purpose of the Act. Section 2(2) explains that the effect of this is that the duty under s 1(1)(b) does not arise, or sometimes does not arise, in relation to that information.

4.8   The next important distinction to grasp is that between those provisions in Pt II that confer absolute exemption, and those that confer non-absolute exemption. Section 2(3) lists the provisions in Pt II that confer absolute exemption. All the provisions in Pt II that are not listed in s 2(3) confer non-absolute exemption.

Absolute exemption

4.9   Where a provision confers absolute exemption, it provides the public authority with a complete answer to any request for information falling within the exemption. There may be scope for argument about whether or not the information sought falls within the relevant exempted category, and any such dispute may be determined by the Commissioner, the Tribunal, or the court, as explained in Ch 5.

Non-absolute exemption

4.10   Where a provision confers non-absolute exemption, there is a difficult balancing exercise to be carried out by the public authority. Section 2 describes this balancing exercise in two slightly different formulations, depending on whether it relates to the duty to confirm or deny, or the duty to communicate. In the case of the duty to confirm or deny, a public authority considering a non-absolute exemption needs to determine whether, in all the circumstances of the case, the public interest in maintaining the exclusion of that duty outweighs the public interest in disclosing whether it holds the information (see s 2(1)(b)). In the case of the duty to communicate, a public authority considering a non-absolute exemption needs to determine whether, in all the circumstances of the case, the public interest in maintaining the exemption outweighs the public interest in disclosure (see s 2(2)(b)).

Public interest

4.11 Therefore, in order to determine whether or not a non-absolute exemption gives grounds for not complying with a request, a public authority has to weigh up the public interest in complying with the relevant FOIA 2000 duty of disclosure, against the public interest in maintaining the relevant FOIA 2000 exemption. Unfortunately, the Act generally does not give any further guidance as to how this balancing exercise is to be carried out.[1] During the Committee Stage of the FOI Bill in the House of Lords, the Minister of State at the Cabinet Office (Lord Falconer of Thoroton) made the following statement about the relationship between the public interest in disclosure and in the maintenance of an exemption—

> 'As far as public interest between disclosure on the one hand and the maintenance of exemption on the other is concerned, it has to be looked at objectively. One looks at the impact of disclosure, that is, making it public. What is the impact of the exemption being maintained? That should be looked at objectively rather than in terms of whatever the motive may be of the person applying. That does not mean that the motive of the person applying may not coincide with factors that could be relevant to what damage may be done and what assistance could be served by making the matter public. But individual motives will not be relevant to that.'.[2]

---

[1] The exception to this is in relation to the exemption in s 35 relating to the formulation of government policy; see paras 4.63, 4.64.
[2] HL Committee Stage, 17 October 2000, col 921.

4.12 One important point to bear in mind is that the balancing exercise is between two different types of *public* interest. Disclosure of information held by public authorities may be thought to be in the public interest because it promotes open and transparent decision-making, or it fosters informed debate on matters of public concern, or it increases public confidence in the institutions of government. However, in a particular case, disclosure may be sought by an individual less for high-minded reasons and more for personal reasons. The applicant may, for example, be seeking information that would be of commercial value to him, or that would assist him in litigation or prospective litigation. It may well be that matters of this sort will be treated as matters of private interest rather than of public interest, and therefore as matters not to be taken into account in carrying out the balancing exercise required by the Act.

4.13 There is, it is suggested, a potential error against which public authorities must guard. Assume that a public authority is considering the application of one of the non-absolute exemptions. It asks itself what weight is to be given, in the circumstances of the case, to the public interest in disclosure, and what weight is to be given to maintaining the exemption. It forms the view that disclosure would have undesirable consequences and, therefore, concludes that there is *no* public interest in disclosure. Hence, there is nothing to set in the balance against the public interest in maintaining the exemption, and inevitably, disclosure will be refused.

4.14 In circumstances such as those described in para 4.13 it is suggested that the public authority has made an error because it has approached the balancing exercise from the wrong starting point. The main purpose of the Act[1] is to implement the principles set out in the White Paper 'Your *Right* to Know',[2] and s 1(1) sets out a general right of access to information. Therefore, the Act assumes that disclosure is, in general, desirable. There will always be some public interest in disclosure and, therefore, there will always be something to be balanced against the public interest in maintaining the exemption.

---

[1]   See FOIA 2000 Explanatory Notes, para 8.
[2]   Cm 3818.

THE SPECIFIC EXEMPTIONS UNDER FOIA 2000

4.15 Part II of the Act (ss 21–44) sets out 23 specific exemptions, based on the subject matter of the request. The table at para 2.8 indicates whether each exemption is absolute or non-absolute.

Information accessible by other means (s 21)

4.16 Information reasonably accessible to the applicant otherwise than by means of a request under FOIA 2000 is exempt information (ie, the duty to communicate does not arise in relation to such information).

Section 21 confers absolute exemption (see s 2(3)(a)). Section 21 does not affect the duty to confirm or deny. Hence, a public authority faced with a request falling under s 21 must still comply with s 1(1)(a) and confirm whether it holds information of the specified description.

4.17　The general duty on a public authority to provide advice and assistance under FOIA 2000, s 16 should also be borne in mind in connection with s 21. Thus, it is suggested that an authority that relies on s 21 ought to take reasonable steps to assist the applicant in identifying what else he can do to obtain the information.

4.18　Information that the public authority, or any other person, is obliged to communicate (otherwise than by making the information available for inspection) under any enactment other than FOIA 2000, will always be taken to be reasonably accessible by means other than a FOIA 2000 request (see s 21(2)(b)).

4.19　Information that is readily accessible to the individual on request from the public authority itself is not to be regarded as being reasonably accessible to the applicant merely for that reason, unless either it falls within s 21(2)(b), or it is made available in accordance with the authority's publication scheme (see s 21(3)).[1]

---

[1]　As to publication schemes, see paras 3.54–3.56.

Information intended for future publication (s 22)

4.20　There is a non-absolute exemption under s 22 in relation to certain information intended for future publication. The terms of the exemption are set out in s 22(1). Section 22(2) provides that the duty to confirm or deny does not arise if, or to the extent that, compliance with that duty would involve the disclosure of information (whether or not already recorded) falling within s 22(1).

4.21　In order to satisfy s 22(1), three conditions must be met—
(1)　The information must be held by the authority with a view to its publication by the authority, or any other person, at some future date (whether determined or not).
(2)　The information must have been held with a view to such publication at the time when the request was made.
(3)　It must be reasonable, in all the circumstances, for the information to be withheld from disclosure until the proposed future publication.

4.22　An example of a situation falling within s 22(1) might be a case where a public authority is carrying out a piece of research with the intention of publishing the research in report form. Section 22(1) might enable the authority to withhold disclosure of the findings of its research until publication of that report.

4.23 This is a non-absolute exemption, therefore even if a request falls within the exemption the public authority must carry out the balancing exercise envisaged by s 2(1)(b) and (2)(b). On the other hand, the request will not even fall within the exemption unless it satisfies s 22(1)(c) (it is reasonable in all the circumstances for the information to be withheld until the date of intended future publication). It is difficult to imagine the exact thought process that public authorities are intended to go through in applying this exemption. It is hard to envisage a situation in which an authority would conclude that withholding the information for the time being was reasonable in all the circumstances, while nevertheless concluding at the same time that the public interest in disclosure outweighed the public interest in applying the exemption. The Act, however, appears to envisage that this is at least a theoretical possibility.

Information relating to security bodies (s 23)

4.24 There are two separate provisions relating to security matters. Section 23 relates to bodies dealing with security matters, and creates an absolute exemption. Section 24 creates a non-absolute exemption relating to security matters more generally.[1]

---

[1] As to s 24, see paras 4.31–4.38.

4.25 Section 23(1) provides that information is exempt if it was directly or indirectly supplied to a public authority by, or relates to, one of a number of specified bodies. The duty to confirm or deny does not arise if, or to the extent that, compliance with that duty would involve the disclosure of information (whether or not already recorded) supplied by, or relating to, one of those specified bodies.

4.26 Section 23(3) lists 12 specified bodies. They include the Security Service, the Secret Intelligence Service, and the Government Communications Headquarters.

4.27 It might be asked why s 23 does not also state that information held by the bodies listed in s 23(3) is also exempt information. The answer is that there is a more fundamental reason why a request directed to any of the s 23(3) bodies would fall outside FOIA 2000. None of those bodies are public bodies for the purpose of the Act, as none of them are listed in Sch 1 to the Act. Thus, if the Security Service passes information about an individual to a government department, that individual cannot obtain the information from either the Security

Service or from the government department concerned. The Security Service is not a public authority within the meaning of the Act and so does not owe any duty under s 1. The government department is a public authority but the information is exempt information in its hands under s 23, and the exemption is absolute.

Certificates under s 23 (s 25)

4.28 Under s 23(2), a certificate signed by a Minister of the Crown stating that information was directly or indirectly supplied by, or relates to, any of the specified bodies, is (subject to s 60) to be taken to be conclusive evidence of that fact. There are a number of other provisions that relate to such certificates. A document purporting to be a certificate under s 23(2) is to be received in evidence and deemed to be such unless the contrary is proved (s 25(1)). A document purporting to be certified by, or on behalf of, a Minister of the Crown as a true copy of such a certificate shall be evidence (in Scotland, sufficient evidence) of that certificate (s 25(2)). The only ministers who can give a certificate under s 23(2) are Cabinet Ministers, the Attorney General, the Advocate General for Scotland or the Attorney General for Northern Ireland (s 25(3)).

4.29 However, the power to issue a certificate under s 23(2) is not absolute. Either the Commissioner or an applicant whose request for information is affected by the issue of the certificate may appeal, under FOIA 2000, s 60(1), to the Tribunal against the issue of the certificate. If the Tribunal finds that the information was not exempt information by virtue of s 23(1), the Tribunal may allow the appeal and quash the certificate (see s 60(2)).

4.30 The Tribunal, therefore, has the power under s 60(2) to substitute its own view for that of the Minister as to whether or not s 23(1) applied to the particular case. The question for the Tribunal is whether s 23(1) was in fact satisfied, and not merely whether the Minister had reasonable grounds for believing that it was satisfied. However, it should be noted that s 60(2) is permissive not mandatory; the Tribunal *may* allow the appeal. This suggests that the Tribunal has some discretion to allow a certificate to stand even if it finds that s 23(1) was not satisfied. It is difficult to see in what circumstances a Tribunal could properly exercise this discretion in favour of allowing the certificate to stand. It is suggested that the only recourse open to a person wishing to challenge such a decision of the Tribunal would be to make an application for judicial review of that decision.

Information relating to national security (s 24)

4.31 Section 24 sets out a more wide-ranging exemption that relates to national security. Information is exempt information if exemption from s 1(1)(b) (the duty to communicate) is required for the purpose of safeguarding national security (s 24(1)). Likewise, the duty to confirm or deny does not arise if, or to the extent that, exemption from s 1(1)(a) is required for the purpose of safeguarding national security (s 24(2)). Unlike the exemption in s 23, this is a non-absolute exemption.

4.32   As with s 23, there is provision under s 24 for a certificate to be signed by a Minister of the Crown (see s 24(3)). A certificate to the effect that exemption from s 1(1)(a) or (b) is, or at any time was, required for the purpose of safeguarding national security is to be conclusive evidence of that fact.[1] A certificate under s 24(3) may be general in description and prospective in effect (s 23(4)).

---
[1]   As with the power to issue certificates under s 23(2), the power to issue them under s 24(3) is subject to s 60; see para 4.35.

Certificate under s 24 (s 25)

4.33   The provisions of s 25 (supplementary provisions in relation to certificates) apply in relation to certificates under s 24(3). Those provisions were discussed in relation to s 23.[1]

---
[1]   See paras 4.28–4.30.

4.34   It is important to note that the effect of a certificate under s 24(3) is different from the effect of a certificate under s 23(2). Section 23 confers an absolute exemption, and so a certificate under s 23(2) will provide a complete answer to an application under FOIA 2000. Section 24 is non-absolute and, therefore, even where there is a certificate in existence under s 24(3), the public authority will need to balance the public interest in disclosure against the public interest in maintaining the exemption, as required by s 2(1)(b) and (2)(b). Interestingly, this balancing exercise is to be carried out by the public authority to which the request is addressed, and not by the Minister who issued the certificate.

Appeal against national security certificate

4.35   The provisions of s 60 apply in relation to certificates issued under s 24(3). The Commissioner, or an applicant whose request for information is affected by the issue of the certificate, may appeal to the Tribunal against the certificate. The Tribunal may allow the appeal and quash the certificate if it finds, applying the principles applied by the court on an application for judicial review, that the Minister did not have reasonable grounds for issuing the certificate (see s 60(3)).

4.36   Thus, the Tribunal cannot simply substitute its own view for that of the Minister as to whether the certificate should have been issued. The

Tribunal will need to consider whether the Minister erred in law (eg, in applying a wrong conception of national security), or took into account irrelevant considerations, or ignored relevant considerations, or reached a decision that no reasonable person could have reached.

4.37   Given that certificates may be general in description and prospective in effect (s 24(4)) it may well be that an applicant will seek to challenge a certificate a long time after it was issued, on the grounds that he has only just made an application that is affected by the certificate. There is nothing in FOIA 2000 to preclude such a challenge to a certificate being brought long after the certificate was issued.

4.38   Alternatively, there may be a dispute between an applicant and a public authority as to whether particular information falls within the general description given in a certificate under s 24(3). The applicant (or indeed any other party to 'proceedings' under FOIA 2000) may appeal to the Tribunal against the public authority's claim that the information falls within the certificate (see s 60(4), (5)).

Defence information (s 26)

4.39   Section 26 provides a wide, but non-absolute, exemption in relation to defence information. Information is exempt information if its disclosure would, or would be likely to, prejudice the defence of the British Islands or of any colony, or the capability, effectiveness or security of the armed forces of the Crown or any forces co-operating with them (see s 26(1), (2)). The duty to confirm or deny does not arise if, or to the extent that, compliance with that duty would, or would be likely to, prejudice any of those matters (s 26(3)).

4.40   There is no provision for the issue of a ministerial certificate in relation to s 26. Thus, the task of determining whether the disclosure of the information sought would be likely to prejudice any of the matters set out in s 26 is a decision to be taken by the public authority to which the request is addressed. As the s 26 exemption is non-absolute, that public authority will also need to balance the public interest in disclosure against the public interest in maintaining the exemption.

4.41   The provision does not require 'substantial prejudice' to the various defence interests set out in s 26, but merely 'prejudice'. On the other hand, as the exemption is non-absolute, the lower the degree of prejudice the more likely it is that the public authority will conclude that the balance of public interest favours disclosure.

4.42   Section 26 does not require that there be active hostilities, or prospective hostilities, at the time when the provision is relied upon. It extends both to the armed forces of the Crown and to forces co-operating with them. It is suggested that this would extend not only to forces that were currently engaged on active service alongside the forces of the Crown, but also to forces engaged in joint military exercises.

International relations (s 27)

4.43   Section 27 sets out a non-absolute exemption relating to international relations. Information is exempt information if its disclosure would, or would be likely to, prejudice a wide range of international interests. Section 27(1) covers relations between the UK and any other state, relations between the UK and any international organisation or international court, the interests of the UK abroad, and the promotion or protection by the UK of its interests abroad. Section 27(2) covers confidential information obtained from a foreign state, an international organisation or an international court. The duty to confirm or deny does not arise to the extent that compliance with that duty would prejudice any of the relations or interests specified in s 27(1), or would involve the disclosure of confidential information as specified in s 27(2) (see s 27(4)).

4.44   The exemption is wide-ranging, and, again, all that is required to bring information within the exemption is prejudice to the specified interests, and not substantial prejudice. However, it is also important to bear in mind that this exemption is not absolute. The public authority considering a request for disclosure will always need to balance the interest in maintaining the exemption against the interest in disclosure. The less significant the prejudice, the more likely it is that the balance will tip in favour of disclosure.

Relations within the UK (s 28)

4.45   Section 28 sets out a non-absolute exemption that reflects the new political landscape in the UK after devolution. Information is exempt if its disclosure would, or would be likely to, prejudice relations between any administration in the UK and any other such administration (s 28(1)). The duty to confirm or deny does not arise if, or to the extent that, compliance with that duty would be likely to prejudice such relations (s 28(3)). There are four relevant administrations—
— the government of the UK,
— the Scottish Administration,
— the Executive Committee of the Northern Ireland Assembly, and
— the National Assembly for Wales (see s 28(2)).

The economy (s 29)

4.46 Section 29 provides for one of the more remarkably drafted exemptions. Section 29(1) provides that information is exempt if its disclosure would, or would be likely to, prejudice the economic interests of the UK or any part thereof, or the financial interests of any administration in the UK.[1] The duty to confirm or deny does not arise if, or to the extent that, compliance would prejudice any of those interests (see s 29(2)).

---

[1] Section 29(1)(b) provides that 'administration in the UK' has the same meaning as in s 28(2); see para 4.45.

4.47 This is a non-absolute exemption, but the drafting is strikingly wide. It is particularly noteworthy that the exemption applies where disclosure would prejudice the interests of a *part* of the UK. Therefore, it is feasible that a local authority could rely on the exemption if it thought that disclosure of the information sought would prejudice the economic interests of its own area.

Investigations and proceedings by public authorities (s 30)

4.48 Section 30 provides for a non-absolute exemption in relation to the conduct of certain legal proceedings by public authorities. There are two categories of exempt information and the duty to confirm or deny does not arise in relation to information falling within either category (see s 30(3)).

4.49 The first category of exempt information under s 30 is defined in s 30(1). Information held by a public authority is exempt if it has at any time been held by the authority for one of three specified purposes. These purposes are—

   (1)   any investigation that the authority has a duty to conduct with a view to ascertaining whether a person should be charged with, or is guilty of, an offence (s 30(1)(a)),

   (2)   any investigation conducted by the authority that may lead to a decision to instigate criminal proceedings which the authority has power to conduct (s 30(1)(b)),

   (3)   any criminal proceedings that the authority has power to conduct (s 30(1)(c)).

4.50 The second category of exempt information under s 30 is defined in s 30(2). Information held by a public authority is exempt if it relates to the obtaining of information from confidential sources, and was obtained, or recorded, for the purposes of one of four sets of functions, namely—

— functions relating to the two sorts of investigations falling within
    s 30(1)(a) or (b) (see s 30(2)(a)(i)),
— functions relating to criminal proceedings that the authority has
    the power to conduct (see s 30(2)(a)(ii)),
— functions relating to investigations conducted for one of the
    purposes set out in s 31(2) (see s 30(2)(a)(iii)),[1] and
— certain civil proceedings arising out of such investigations (see
    s 30(2)(a)(iv)).

---

[1] As to s 31(2), see para 4.52.

4.51   The purpose of the exemption in s 30 is to protect certain functions
relating to the conduct of legal proceedings, especially criminal
proceedings. Some of the drafting is, at first sight, obscure. For instance,
what is the difference between cases that fall within s 30(1)(a) or (b),
and cases that fall within s 30(2)(a)(i)? The difference is actually quite
important. Unlike s 30(1), s 30(2) only applies in relation to the
obtaining of information from confidential sources. In other words, the
difference is that s 30(1)(a) and (b) cover information held for the
purposes of certain investigations, whereas s 30(2)(a)(i) covers
information obtained, or recorded, for the purposes of *functions relating
to* those investigations. Information obtained in the course of a specific
criminal investigation would, it is suggested, fall within s 30(1)(a) or (b),
whereas information obtained in order to cast light on the way in which
a public authority was discharging its functions in relation to criminal
investigations generally would fall within s 30(2)(a)(i).

Law enforcement (s 31)

4.52   Section 31 creates a non-absolute exemption in relation to a long list of
law enforcement functions. Information which is not exempt
information by virtue of s 30 is exempt if its disclosure would, or would
be likely to, prejudice any of the matters specified in s 31(1). The
matters specified in s 31(1) are widely drafted and include the
prevention or detection of crime, the apprehension and prosecution of
offenders, the administration of justice, and the operation of
immigration controls. Section 31(1) also exempts information that
would, or would be likely to, prejudice the exercise by a public
authority of its functions for any of the purposes specified in s 30(2). It
further exempts information that would, or would be likely to,
prejudice civil proceedings brought by an authority arising out of
investigations conducted for the purposes set out in that subsection.
The purposes set out in s 31(2) are wide-ranging and include:
investigations into whether circumstances exist justifying regulatory
action under any enactment; regulatory investigations relating to
unfitness or incompetence of company directors; investigation of
persons in regulated professions or who carry out activities that require

a licence; investigations into accidents, and actions relating to health and safety; action relating to the management of charities. The duty to confirm or deny does not arise if, or to the extent, that compliance with the duty would, or would be likely to, prejudice any of the matters mentioned in s 31(1).

Court records, etc (s 32)

4.53 Section 32 creates an absolute exemption relating to court records. Information falling within s 32 is exempt information, and the duty to confirm or deny does not arise in relation to such information.

4.54 Section 32 covers information that is held only by virtue of being contained in certain types of document. This includes documents filed with a court for the purposes of court proceedings, documents served upon, or by, a public authority for the purposes of court proceedings, or documents created by a court or a member of its administrative staff for the purposes of court proceedings.

4.55 It is important to bear in mind that information is exempt if it is held *only* by virtue of being contained in a document of the type specified. Assume that a public authority is being sued. The authority will hold copies of the pleadings in the case. Information that is contained in the pleadings and nowhere else will be protected by the absolute exemption in s 32. However, information that is held elsewhere by the public authority may well be liable to disclosure (depending on whether it falls within any of the other exemptions in FOIA 2000).

Audit functions (s 33)

4.56 Section 33 creates a non-absolute exemption in relation to information the disclosure of which would, or would be likely to, prejudice the exercise of a public authority's functions of a particular type, and the duty to confirm or deny does not arise if, or to the extent that, its disclosure would, or would be likely to, prejudice the exercise of those functions. The particular functions to which s 33(1) applies are functions in relation to the audit of the accounts of other public authorities, or the examination of the economy, efficiency and effectiveness with which other public authorities use their resources in discharging their functions.

4.57 Section 33 applies where public authorities exercise audit, or audit-related, functions in respect of other public authorities. It does not apply in relation to a public authority's audit of its own accounts, or examination of the efficiency of its own use of resources.

Parliamentary privilege (s 34)

4.58   Section 34 creates an absolute exemption in relation to Parliamentary privilege. There is an exemption from both the duty to communicate and the duty to confirm or deny, to the extent that exemption is required in order to avoid an infringement of the privileges of either House of Parliament (see s 34(1), (2)). A certificate signed by the Speaker of the House of Commons (in relation to that House) or by the Clerk of the Parliaments (in relation to the House of Lords) is to be conclusive evidence that exemption is required in a particular case in order to avoid such infringement (see s 34(3), (4)). Note that there is no mechanism for challenging such a certificate (compare this with the provisions of s 60, under which a ministerial certificate in relation to security matters and national security issued under ss 23(2) or 24(3) may be challenged on appeal to the Tribunal).[1]

---

[1]   See paras 4.29, 4.30, 4.35–4.38.

Formulation of government policy (s 35)

4.59   Section 35 is the first of two widely drafted, and controversial, exemptions intended to protect the process of policy formation from scrutiny under FOIA 2000. At the outset, it is important to bear in mind that s 35 does not create an absolute exemption. Hence, the public authority to which the request is directed will need to balance the public interest in disclosure against the public interest in maintaining this exemption, in order to decide whether, on the facts of the particular case, the exemption bars disclosure. Section 35 is the only exemption in relation to which there is any specific guidance as to how this balancing exercise is to be carried out.[1]

---

[1]   See paras 4.63, 4.64.

4.60   Under s 35, information is exempt information if it falls into one of four categories specified in s 35(1), and the duty to confirm or deny does not arise in relation to information falling within those categories (see s 35(3)). Information held by a government department or the National Assembly for Wales is exempt under s 35(1) if it relates to—
    —   the formulation or development of government policy (s 35(1)(a)),
    —   ministerial communications (s 35(1)(b)),
    —   the provision of advice by the Law Officers or any request for the provision of such advice (s 35(1)(c)), or
    —   the operation of any ministerial private office (s 35(1)(d)).

4.61   One of the most important policy choices that had to be made in framing the Act was how far FOIA 2000 should require disclosure of the process of policy formulation? There were competing considerations. On the one hand, disclosure might be thought to promote informed public debate. On the other hand, it might be suggested that the prospect of disclosure would inhibit discussion within government. At first sight, s 35 comes down firmly against disclosure.

4.62 There are, however, two provisions in s 35 that mitigate the effect of s 35(1). Section 35(2) provides that once a decision as to government policy has been taken, then any statistical information used to provide an informed background to the taking of the decision is not to be regarded as relating to the formation or development of government policy, nor as relating to ministerial communications. Section 35(2), therefore, removes from the scope of the exemption created by s 35(1) certain information that would at first sight fall within that subsection. Section 35(2) is, however, limited in scope. It only applies to statistical information. Moreover, it only applies once a decision has been taken.

4.63 Section 35(4) also mitigates the effect of s 35(1)(a), using a technique not found elsewhere in the Act. It states that in making the determination required by s 2(1)(b) or (2)(b) (that is to say, in balancing the public interest in maintaining the exemption against the public interest in disclosure) regard is to be had to the particular public interest in the disclosure of factual information which has been used, or is intended to be used, to provide an informed background to decision-taking.

4.64 This is the only provision in FOIA 2000 that gives specific guidance as to how the balancing exercise required in relation to non-absolute exemptions is to be carried out. Section 35(4) assumes that it is possible to draw a distinction between policy advice, and factual information upon which that advice is based. It gives a clear signal to public authorities that they should be ready to disclose the latter, whether the information relates to decisions that have been taken or to decisions that are still to be taken. However, even if information falls within s 35(4) there is no guarantee of disclosure, as it remains open to a public authority to conclude that the balance of public interest in a particular case is in favour of maintaining the exemption created by s 35(1). It should be noted that during the Third Reading of the FOI Bill in the House of Lords, the Minister of State at the Cabinet Office stated—

> 'I also emphasise that the government believe that factual information used to provide an informed background to decision-taking will normally be disclosed.'.[1]

---

[1]   HL 3R, 24 October 2000, col 297.

Prejudice to effective conduct of public affairs (s 36)

4.65 Section 36 creates another wide-ranging exemption, intended to protect the conduct of public affairs from excessive scrutiny under

FOIA 2000. The exemption is non-absolute, except in so far as relating to information held by either House of Parliament.

4.66 Section 36 applies to information held by a government department or the National Assembly for Wales which is not exempt information by virtue of s 35, and information held by any other public authority. Under s 36(2), information is exempt information if, in the reasonable opinion of a qualified person,[1] its disclosure would have certain specified effects. Likewise, the duty to confirm or deny does not arise if, or to the extent that, compliance with that duty would have any of those effects.

---

[1]   As to the meaning of qualified person, see para 4.69.

4.67 The effects that s 36 seeks to avoid are set out in s 36(2). The first of these is prejudice, or likely prejudice, to the maintenance of the convention of collective responsibility of Ministers of the Crown, to the work of the Executive Committee of the Northern Ireland Assembly, and to the work of the executive committee of the National Assembly for Wales (s 36(2)(a)). The second is the inhibition, or likely inhibition, of the free and frank provision of advice or the free and frank exchange of views for the purposes of deliberation (s 36(2)(b)). The third is prejudice, or likely prejudice, to the effective conduct of public affairs (s 36(2)(c)).

4.68 Information only falls within this exemption if 'in the reasonable opinion of a qualified person' compliance with the duties imposed by FOIA 2000 would have the specified effects. This 'reasonable opinion' requirement does not apply in relation to statistical information (see s 36(4)).

4.69 There are elaborate provisions in s 36(5) defining 'qualified person' for the purposes of this section.[1] For instance, in the case of information held by a government department in the charge of a Minister of the Crown, any Minister of the Crown (not necessarily the one in charge of the department) will be a qualified person (s 36(5)(a)).

---

[1]   Section 36(5) actually sets out 15 separate meanings of this term depending on the circumstances.

4.70 There are special provisions for the protection of information held by either House of Parliament. A certificate signed by the Speaker of the House of Commons (in relation to information held by that House) or by the Clerk of the Parliaments (in relation to information held by the House of Lords) is to be conclusive evidence that compliance with the duty to communicate, or the duty to confirm or deny would, or would be likely to, have any of the effects specified in s 36(2). Moreover, in relation to information held by either House of Parliament the exemption conferred by s 36 is absolute (see s 2(3)(e)).

4.71 Leaving aside the special case of information held by either House of Parliament, s 36 at first sight appears to be a very wide limitation on the general principle of free access to information laid down in s 1(1). However, three points should be noted—

    (1)   The exemption does not operate at all unless the qualified person, as defined in s 36(5), is of the reasonable opinion that s 36(2) is satisfied.

    (2)   The exemption is non-absolute. Thus, the balance between the public interest in disclosure and the public interest in maintaining the exemption must be considered. This should be done by the public authority to which the request is directed, not by the qualified person who determines the question set out in s 36(2).

    (3)   The opinion of the qualified person must be reasonable.

4.72 What if the qualified person expresses an opinion that is unreasonable? How should that expression of opinion be challenged? There are two possibilities. One is an application for judicial review. An alternative is to appeal to the Commissioner if the application is refused. It remains to be seen whether the courts will entertain an application for judicial review or whether they will treat the appeal to the Commissioner as the sole permissible basis of challenge.

Communications with Her Majesty, etc (s 37)

4.73 Section 37 creates a narrow, non-absolute exemption. Information relating to communications with Her Majesty or other members of the Royal family or the Royal household, or relating to the conferring by the Crown of any honour or dignity, is exempt information (s 37(1)). The duty to confirm or deny does not arise in relation to information which is exempt under this section (s 37(2)).

Health and safety (s 38)

4.74 Section 38 creates a non-absolute exemption in relation to health and safety. Information is exempt if its disclosure under the Act would, or would be likely to, endanger the physical or mental health of any individual, or endanger the safety of any individual (s 38(1)). The duty to confirm or deny does not arise if, or to the extent that, compliance with that duty would be likely to have either effect (s 38(2)).

Environmental information (s 39)

4.75 Section 39 creates a non-absolute exemption in relation to environmental information. The purpose of this exemption is to ensure that disclosure of certain environmental information is governed by any regulations made in order to implement the Aarhus Convention,[1] and not by the general provisions of FOIA 2000. Section 74(3) of FOIA 2000 provides that the Secretary of State may, by regulations, make such provision as he considers appropriate for implementing the information provisions of the Aarhus Convention.[2] Any regulations made under this power will replace the Environmental Information Regulations 1992.[3]

---

[1]   The Convention on access to information, public participation in decision-making and access to justice in environmental matters (Aarhus, 25 June 1998).
[2]   These are defined in FOIA 2000, s 74(2) as Art 4, and Arts 3 and 9 in so far as relating to that Article.
[3]   SI 1992/3240.

4.76   Under s 39(1), information is exempt information if the public authority holding it is obliged by regulations under s 74 to make it available to the public in accordance with the regulations, or would be so obliged but for any exemption contained in the regulations. The duty to confirm or deny does not arise in relation to such information (see s 39(2)).

Personal information (s 40)

4.77   Section 40 contains an elaborate series of exemptions, the purpose of which is to address the potential overlap between FOIA 2000 and the Data Protection Act 1998. Some of these exemptions are absolute, and some are qualified.

4.78   Section 40(1) creates an absolute exemption. Information is exempt information if it is personal data and the applicant for that information is the data subject. The terms 'personal data' and 'data subject' have the same meaning as in the Data Protection Act 1998, s 1(1) (see s 40(7)).[1] Where information is exempt under s 40(1), the duty to confirm or deny does not arise in relation to that information (see s 40(5)(a)).

---

[1]   Section 1(1) of the Data Protection Act 1998 provides that 'personal data' means data which relate to a living individual who can be identified from those data, or from those data and other information which is in the possession of, or is likely to come into the possession of, the data controller, and includes any expression of opinion about the individual and any indication of the intentions of the data controller or any other person in respect of the individual. A 'data subject' is an individual who is the subject of personal data.

4.79   Section 40(2) creates a further exemption which is absolute in part. Information which does not fall within s 40(1) is exempt information if either the condition set out in s 40(3) is satisfied or the condition set out in s 40(4) is satisfied. These are referred to as 'the first condition' and 'the second condition' respectively.

4.80   The first condition (s 40(3)) breaks down into two limbs. The first limb is set out in s 40(3)(a). This applies in a case where the information falls within any of paras (a)–(d) of the definition of 'data' in the Data

Protection Act 1998, s 1(1).[1] In cases falling within this limb of s 40(3), the first condition is satisfied where the disclosure to a member of the public other than under FOIA 2000 would contravene any of the data protection principles set out in the Data Protection Act 1998 (see s 40(3)(a)(i)), or would contravene s 10 of that Act (s 40(3)(a)(ii)). The second limb is set out in s 40(3)(b). This applies in a case falling outside s 40(3)(a) (that is, a case where the information does not fall within any of paras (a)–(d) of the definition of data in s 1(1) of the 1998 Act). Where this limb applies, the condition is satisfied if the disclosure of the information to a member of the public other than under FOIA 2000 would contravene any of the data protection principles if the exemptions in s 33A(1) of the 1998 Act (relating to manual data held by public authorities) were disregarded.

---

[1]   The relevant part of this definition is as follows—
'"data" means information which—
- (a)   is being processed by means of equipment operating automatically in response to instructions given for that purpose,
- (b)   is recorded with the intention that it should be processed by means of such equipment,
- (c)   is recorded as part of a relevant filing system or with the intention that it should form part of a relevant filing system, or
- (d)   does not fall within paragraph (a), (b) or (c) but forms part of an accessible record as defined by section 68.'

4.81   The second condition is set out in s 40(4). This condition is satisfied if the information requested is exempted from the Data Protection Act 1998, s 7(1)(c) (data subject's right of access to personal data) by virtue of any provision of Pt IV of that Act.

4.82   The exemption created by FOIA 2000, s 40(2) is absolute in so far as relating to cases where the first condition is satisfied by virtue of s 40(3)(a)(i) or (b) (see s 2(3)(f)(ii)).

4.83   Section 40(5)(b) creates a wide exemption from the duty to confirm or deny. This exemption is non-absolute. The duty does not arise if, or to the extent that, compliance with that duty would contravene any of the data protection principles, or the Data Protection Act 1998, s 10, or would do so if the exemptions in s 33A(1) of that Act were disregarded. Further, the duty does not arise if, by virtue of any provision of the Data Protection Act 1998, Pt IV, the information is exempt from s 7(1)(a) of that Act (data subject's right to be informed whether personal data is being processed).

Information provided in confidence (s 41)

4.84   Section 41 creates an absolute exemption, but only in relation to an actionable breach of confidence. Under this section, information is exempt if it was obtained by the public authority from another person (including another public authority), and the disclosure of the information by the authority would constitute an actionable breach of confidence (s 41(1)). It does not matter whether the breach of confidence would be actionable by the person who provided the information, or by some other person. The duty to confirm or deny does not arise if compliance with that duty would give rise to an actionable breach of confidence (s 41(2)).

4.85 The scope of this exemption will depend on the future development of the tort of breach of confidence. This is a developing area of law following the commencement of the Human Rights Act 1998.

Legal professional privilege (s 42)

4.86 Surprisingly perhaps, the exemption created by s 42 in relation to this subject matter is non-absolute. Information in respect of which a claim to legal professional privilege[1] could be maintained in legal proceedings is confidential information (s 42(1)). The duty to confirm or deny does not arise if, or to the extent that, compliance with that duty would involve the disclosure of any such information (s 42(2)).

---

[1]   Or in Scotland, confidentiality of communications.

Commercial interests (s 43)

4.87 Section 43 creates two non-absolute exemptions intended to protect commercial interests. First, information is exempt if it constitutes a trade secret (s 43(1)). Secondly, information is exempt if its disclosure would, or would be likely to, prejudice the commercial interests of any person (including the public authority holding it) (see s 43(2)). The duty to confirm or deny does not arise if, or to the extent that, compliance with that duty would, or would be likely to, prejudice the interests mentioned in sub-s (2) (s 43(3)).

4.88 The striking feature of this exemption is that it protects the commercial interests of any person, and not merely of the public authority holding the information. Thus, the exemption protects purely private commercial interests. This raises interesting questions for public authorities seeking to balance the public interest in maintaining this exemption (which is a non-absolute exemption) against the public interest in disclosure. There will in many cases be a strong private commercial interest in resisting disclosure. It is doubtful whether this is something to which public authorities should have regard in deciding whether this exemption bars disclosure.

4.89 It is suggested that the exemption in s 43(2) is likely to be of importance in cases where commercially sensitive information (not amounting to a trade secret and so not falling within s 43(1)) is entrusted to a public authority. Disclosure of such information may inhibit the free flow of similar information to the public authority in the future. This is a matter of public interest, and can properly be taken into account in determining whether the exemption bars disclosure in a particular case. On the other hand, the harm that may be done to private commercial interests by disclosure will often be a matter of private rather than public interest, and so will not in itself be something to be taken into account in carrying out the statutory balancing exercise.

Prohibitions on disclosure (s 44)

4.90 There is an absolute exemption in relation to information the disclosure of which (otherwise than under FOIA 2000 itself) is prohibited under any enactment, is incompatible with any Community obligation, or would constitute or be punishable as a contempt of court (s 44(1)). The duty to confirm or deny does not arise if the confirmation or denial would fall within s 44(1) (see s 44(2)).

5 Codes of practice, enforcement and appeals

PROMOTING GOOD PRACTICE

5.1 The Secretary of State, the Lord Chancellor and the Information Commissioner are all given a role under FOIA 2000, Pt III (ss 45–49) in promoting good practice in relation to the disclosure of information by public authorities. However, it should be noted that responsibility for freedom of information and data protection was transferred from the Home Office to the Lord Chancellor's Department; see the Transfer of Functions (Miscellaneous) Order 2001, SI 2001/3500. Hence, the functions conferred on the Secretary of State by FOIA 2000 will, in practice, now be exercised by the Lord Chancellor.

Secretary of State

5.2 Under FOIA 2000, s 45(1), the Secretary of State[1] is required to issue a code of practice providing guidance to public authorities as to the practice which, in his opinion, it would be desirable for them to follow in connection with the discharge of their functions under FOIA 2000, Pt I.[2] The code must include provision relating to certain matters set out in s 45(2), namely—
   — the provision of advice and assistance to persons requesting information;
   — the transfer of requests between public authorities;
   — consultation with persons to whom the information requested relates or persons whose interests are likely to be affected by its disclosure;
   — the inclusion in contracts entered into by public authorities of terms relating to the disclosure of information; and
   — complaints procedures.

---

[1] Now the Lord Chancellor; see the Transfer of Functions (Miscellaneous) Order 2001, SI 2001/3500.
[2] A draft code of practice on the discharge of functions under the Act is the subject of consultation at the time of writing; see Appendix 2.

5.3 The reference to consultation raises an interesting question. Assume that a public body decides to release information in response to a request under FOIA 2000, without consulting a person whose interests are affected by the disclosure. Assume further, that this failure is a breach of the code, and that the person whose interests are affected would have wished to have had an opportunity to persuade the public authority not to release the information. What remedies are open to the person affected?

5.4   It is suggested that the person affected would not be able to apply to the Commissioner under s 50 for a decision as to whether the request for information had been dealt with in accordance with the requirements of FOIA 2000, Pt I.[1] The complaint would not be that the requirements of Pt I had been breached, but rather, that the provisions of a code of practice under Pt III had been breached.

---

[1]   As to s 50, see para 5.14 et seq.

5.5   If the decision to release information had been taken, but the information had not yet been released, it may be that the person affected would be able to challenge the decision to release the information in an application for judicial review. However, once the information had actually been released, it is difficult to see how such a challenge could succeed, as there would be no point in giving any remedy.

The Lord Chancellor

5.6   The Lord Chancellor is required to issue a code of practice under FOIA 2000, s 46(1), providing guidance to 'relevant authorities' as to the practice which, in his opinion, it would be desirable for them to follow in connection with the keeping, management and destruction of their records.[1] 'Relevant authorities' means any public authority, and any other office or body whose administrative and departmental records are public records for the purpose of the Public Records Act 1958 or the Public Records Act (Northern Ireland) 1923 (see s 46(7)). The code may also give guidance in relation to the transfer of records under the 1958 and 1923 Acts, and in relation to the practice of reviewing records before they are transferred under those provisions (s 46(2)).

---

[1]   A draft code of practice on records management is the subject of consultation at the time of writing; see Appendix 2.

The Information Commissioner

5.7   The Information Commissioner's role under FOIA 2000 is complex. The Commissioner has an enforcement role under FOIA 2000, Pt IV,[1] and a role in promoting best practice under FOIA 2000, Pt III.

---

[1]   As to enforcement, see para 5.12 et seq.

5.8   Under s 47(1) the Commissioner has a general duty to promote good practice by public authorities, and to promote the observance by those authorities of the requirements of FOIA 2000 and the provisions of the codes of practice under ss 45 and 46. The Commissioner is required to arrange for the dissemination of information to the public about FOIA 2000 itself, good practice, and his own functions (see s 47(2)), and he may give advice on any of those matters. He may also (under s 47(3)) assess, with the consent of any public authority, whether that authority is following good practice. The Commissioner may charge for services provided under s 47 and the sums charged are to be determined by him with the consent of the Secretary of State (s 47(4)).

5.9   It should be noted that for the purposes of s 47 'good practice' includes, but is not limited to, compliance with FOIA 2000 and with the codes issued under ss 45 and 46 (s 47(6)).

Recommendations as to good practice

5.10   Under s 48(1), the Commissioner may give a 'practice recommendation' to a public authority if it appears that the practice of that authority does not conform with the codes made under ss 45 and 46. A practice recommendation must refer to the particular provisions of the relevant code with which, in the Commissioner's opinion, the practice of the relevant public authority does not conform (s 48(2)).

Annual report

5.11   The Commissioner is required annually to lay a general report on the exercise of his functions under FOIA 2000 before each House of Parliament (s 49(1)).

ENFORCEMENT

5.12   Part IV (ss 50–56) of FOIA 2000 deals with enforcement, and Pt V (ss 57–61) deals with appeals. The structure of the Act provides that the Information Commissioner bears the main responsibility for enforcement, with an appellate role for the Information Tribunal and the courts.

5.13   Part IV confers power on the Commissioner to issue three sorts of notice on a public authority, ie, a decision notice, an information notice, and an enforcement notice. Where a public authority fails to comply with any of these notices, the Commissioner may certify that failure to the court, which may deal with the authority as if it had committed a contempt of court.[1] There is one important limitation on the powers of the Commissioner. Section 53 of the Act gives 'the accountable person' (in practice a Cabinet minister or person of similar status) the power to override decision notices or enforcement notices relating to information that falls within any of the exemptions in FOIA 2000, Pt II.[2]

---

[1] Ie, under s 54; see para 5.31.
[2] See para 5.25 et seq.

Decision notices

5.14 Any person (referred to for this purpose as 'the complainant') may apply to the Commissioner under s 50(1) for a decision as to whether, in any specified respect, a request for information made by the complainant to a public authority has been dealt with in accordance with the requirements of Pt I.

5.15 Note that the complainant must be a person who has requested information from a public authority. Hence, if X applies to a public authority for disclosure of information affecting Y's commercial interests, and the public authority refuses disclosure, X can apply to the Commissioner for a decision under s 50(1). However, if the public authority grants disclosure, Y cannot make an application. It appears that the only way in which Y could challenge the decision to grant disclosure would be by an application for judicial review.

5.16 There are four circumstances in which the Commissioner is not required to make any decision in relation to a s 50(1) application. He may refuse if it appears to him that—
    (1)   the complainant has not exhausted any complaints procedure provided by the public authority,[1]
    (2)   there has been undue delay,
    (3)   the application is frivolous or vexatious,
    (4)   the application has been withdrawn or abandoned (s 50(2)).

Otherwise, he must serve a decision notice on the complainant and the public authority. Where the Commissioner decides that the public authority has failed to comply with the duty to confirm or deny, or the duty to communicate information under s 1(1), or has failed to comply with ss 11 or 17,[2] the decision notice must specify the steps to be taken to comply with the requirement and the period within which those steps are to be taken (s 50(4)).

---

[1] Ie, the complaints procedure provided by the public authority in conformity with the code of practice under s 45.
[2] As to ss 11 and 17, see paras 2.20 and 3.44 et seq, respectively.

Information notices

5.17   Section 51 of the Act makes provision for the Commissioner to serve information notices on public authorities.

5.18   An information notice may be served in three circumstances (s 51(1)). The first is where the Commissioner has received an application under s 50. The second is where the Commissioner reasonably requires information in order to decide whether a public authority has complied, or is complying, with any of the requirements of Pt I. The third is for the purpose of determining whether the public authority is complying with any codes of practice under ss 45 or 46.

5.19   The information notice will require the public authority to furnish the Commissioner with such information as is specified in that notice, within the time specified in that notice. Section 51(5) provides some protection in relation to legal professional privilege. A public authority shall not be required to furnish the Commissioner with any information in respect of any communication between a professional legal adviser and his client in connection with the giving of advice to the client concerning FOIA 2000. This is also the case in respect of any communication between adviser and client, or between adviser or client and any other person, made in connection with, or in contemplation of, proceedings under FOIA 2000. Note however, that there is no protection for legal professional privilege where the advice, or the contemplated litigation, does not relate to FOIA 2000 itself.

Enforcement notices

5.20   If the Commissioner is satisfied that a public authority has failed to comply with any of the requirements of FOIA 2000, Pt I, he may serve the authority with an enforcement notice specifying the steps that the authority must take to comply with the Act, and the period within which they must be taken (see s 52(1)).

5.21   Note that an enforcement notice can be issued by the Commissioner without any person having made a complaint to the Commissioner.

Scope of the Commissioner's powers

5.22   The most important of the Commissioner's powers is his power to require a public authority to disclose information, either of his own motion (by enforcement notice) or in response to a complaint from a person seeking information (by decision notice). If the public authority still refuses to disclose the information, ultimately the matter can be dealt with as if it was a contempt of court.[1]

---

[1]   Ie, under s 54; see para 5.31.

5.23 The exemptions set out in FOIA 2000, Pt II require public authorities to exercise judgment in two ways. First, as to whether or not the exemption applies at all, which may require a decision as to whether the exemption is needed in order to avoid the risk of specified sorts of harm. Secondly, in the case of non-absolute exemptions, they will need to exercise judgment as to whether the public interest in maintaining the exemption outweighs the public interest in disclosing the information. The Commissioner has power to substitute his own judgment for that of a public authority in respect of both kinds of question, by ordering that information be disclosed in a case where the public authority has refused disclosure in reliance on one of the exemptions. There is, however, one very serious qualification to this. Section 53 allows certain categories of decision notice or enforcement notice to be overridden, on behalf of the public authority concerned, by the accountable person.[1]

---

[1] See para 5.25 et seq.

Appeals

5.24 In relation to all three types of notice, there are provisions for appeal to the Information Tribunal under FOIA 2000, s 57 (see paras 5.35–5.39). Each notice must give particulars of the right of appeal under s 57 (see s 50(5) in relation to decision notices, s 51(3) in relation to information notices, and s 52(2)(b) in relation to enforcement notices). The specified period within which steps must be taken under any of the notices must not expire before the end of the period within which an appeal can be brought. Furthermore, the bringing of an appeal will operate as a stay on the duty to comply with the notice (see ss 50(6), 51(4) and 52(3)).

Exceptions from duty to comply

5.25 Under s 53, the effect of certain decision notices or enforcement notices can be overridden by the 'accountable person'. Note that s 53 does not apply in relation to information notices.

5.26 Section 53 applies to decision notices or enforcement notices served on a government department, the National Assembly for Wales, or any public authority designated for the purposes of this section by an order made by the Secretary of State (s 53(1)(a)). It applies if, and only if, the decision notice or enforcement notice relates to a failure to comply with s 1(1) in respect of information which falls within any provision of Pt II stating that the duty to confirm or deny does not apply, or in respect of exempt information (s 53(1)(b)).

5.27 In other words, s 53 applies in relation to decision or enforcement notices that relate to information falling within one of the absolute or non-absolute exemptions set out in FOIA 2000, Pt II. In effect, it enables the accountable person to override the Commissioner's judgment as to whether or not any of those exemptions apply. Section 53(2) states that a decision or enforcement notice to which the section applies shall cease to have effect if the accountable person, in relation to the public authority in question, certifies to the Commissioner, in writing, that he has formed the opinion on reasonable grounds that, in respect of the request or requests concerned, there was no failure to comply with the Act. A certificate under s 53(2) must be given to the Commissioner not later than the twentieth working day following the 'effective date' (ie, the date when the notice was given to the public authority, or, where there is an appeal under s 57, the date when the appeal is determined or withdrawn (see s 53(4)).

5.28 A copy of a certificate under s 53(2) must be laid before each House of Parliament. It must also be laid before the Northern Ireland Assembly (in cases relating to a Northern Ireland department or public authority) and the National Assembly for Wales (in cases relating to that Assembly or any Welsh public authority) (see s 53(3)). If the certificate relates to a decision notice, the accountable person must inform the person who was the complainant for the purposes of s 50 of the reasons for his decision, unless to do so would involve the disclosure of exempt information (s 53(6), (7)).

5.29 The term 'accountable person' is defined in s 53(8). In relation to a Northern Ireland department or any Northern Ireland public authority, it means the First Minister and deputy First Minister in Northern Ireland, acting jointly. In relation to the National Assembly for Wales or any Welsh public authority, it means the Assembly First Secretary. In relation to any other public authority it means a Cabinet minister, the Attorney General, the Advocate General for Scotland or the Attorney General for Northern Ireland.

5.30 Section 53 provides a very significant limitation on the power of the Commissioner to enforce FOIA 2000. What it means is that, in relation to public bodies falling within s 53(1)(a), the final judgment as to whether or not any of the Pt II exemptions applies rests in the hands of the executive and not in the hands of the Commissioner. It is, however, suggested that any decision to issue a certificate under s 53 would be susceptible to challenge by way of judicial review.

Failure to comply with notice

5.31 Section 54 of the Act contains the most important sanction available to the Commissioner. Where a public authority has failed to comply with an information or enforcement notice, or with so much of a decision notice as requires steps to be taken, the Commissioner may certify that failure to the court. The court may inquire into the matter and, after hearing witnesses against or on behalf of the public authority and any statement offered in defence, may deal with the authority as if it had committed a contempt of court. For the purposes of this section, 'court' means the High Court or the Court of Session (s 54(4)).

POWERS OF ENTRY AND INSPECTION

5.32 Section 55 of the Act introduces Sch 3 which contains provisions relating to powers of entry and inspection. A circuit judge may grant a warrant to the Commissioner authorising him (or any of his officers or staff) to enter and search premises, inspect and seize documents or other materials, and inspect equipment in which information held by a public authority may be recorded (Sch 3, para 1(2)). In order to obtain a warrant the Commissioner must provide evidence on oath as to two matters, namely that there are reasonable grounds for suspecting that—

(1) a public authority is failing, or has failed, to comply with FOIA 2000, Pt I, or with a decision notice, an information notice or an enforcement notice, or that an offence under s 77 has been, or is being, committed (Sch 3, para 1(1)(a));[1] and

(2) relevant evidence is to be found on the premises to be searched (Sch 3, para 1(1)(b)).

---

[1] The offence under s 77 relates to the alteration, etc, of records with the intent to prevent disclosure; see para 6.12 et seq.

5.33 In general, the Commissioner must seek access by agreement before obtaining a warrant, and the occupier of the premises must be given an opportunity to be heard before the warrant is issued. However, these provisions do not apply if the judge is satisfied that the case is urgent, or that compliance would defeat the object of the entry (Sch 3, para 2). Schedule 3 also contains detailed provisions as to the execution of warrants (see Sch 3, paras 4–7). It is an offence intentionally to obstruct a person in the execution of a warrant, or to fail without reasonable excuse to give any person executing a warrant such assistance as he may reasonably require (Sch 3, para 12). A government department is not liable to prosecution under FOIA 2000, but Sch 3, para 12 applies to a person in the public service of the Crown, or to a person acting on behalf of either House of Parliament or of the Northern Ireland Assembly, in the same way as it would apply to any other person (see s 81(3), (4)).

NO ACTION AGAINST PUBLIC AUTHORITY

5.34   Section 56 provides that FOIA 2000 confers no right of action in civil proceedings. This provision is stated not to affect the powers of the Commissioner under s 54.

APPEALS

5.35   Part V (ss 57–61) of the Act confers an appellate jurisdiction on the Information Tribunal (the Tribunal: previously known as the Data Protection Tribunal) (see s 18(2)).

5.36   The Tribunal has an appellate jurisdiction under s 57 in relation to decision notices, information notices and enforcement notices. In relation to decision notices, either the complainant or the public authority may appeal to the Tribunal. In relation to information notices or enforcement notices, the public authority may appeal.

Exceptions

5.37   Four important limitations on these rights of appeal to the Tribunal should be noted—
  (1) there is no appeal against a decision by the Commissioner not to serve an information notice or an enforcement notice;
  (2) there is no appeal against a decision by the Commissioner not to certify to the court under s 54 a failure by a public authority to comply with a notice;
  (3) there is no appeal against the exercise by the accountable person of the power under FOIA 2000, s 53 to override the effect of a decision notice or enforcement notice;
  (4) only the complainant (who will be a person requesting information from a public body under s 50) and the public authority have a right of appeal to the Tribunal (s 57(1)). If the Commissioner proposes to compel A (a public authority) to disclose to B (the person requesting information) material that relates to C (a third party), then C has no right of appeal to the Tribunal.

Any challenge in relation to any of these four matters would have to be brought by way of an application for judicial review, not by appeal to the Tribunal.

Determination of appeals

5.38 Although the Tribunal's jurisdiction on appeal is limited in the respects set out at para 5.37, its powers in relation to those appeals that it has jurisdiction to entertain are very wide. Under s 58 the Tribunal may do one of three things. It may dismiss the appeal (s 58(2)). It may allow the appeal (which must mean that the notice under appeal is quashed, though curiously the section does not say so in such terms) (s 58(1)). It may also substitute, for the original notice, such other notice as the Commissioner could have served (s 58(1)). The Tribunal can quash or vary a notice on two grounds, ie, that the Tribunal considers that the notice was not in accordance with the law (s 58(1)(a)), or that, to the extent that the notice involved an exercise of discretion by the Commissioner, it considers that he ought to have exercised his discretion differently (s 58(1)(b)). The Tribunal may review any finding of fact on which the notice was based (s 58(2)).

5.39 It remains to be seen how broadly the Tribunal interprets these powers of appeal. In relation to the exercise of any discretion by the Commissioner, the question arises as to whether the Tribunal can simply substitute its own view for that of the Commissioner, or whether it can it do so only where the Commissioner reached a decision that was not reasonable. It is suggested that the actual language of s 58(1) ('... the Tribunal considers ... that he ought to have exercised his discretion differently ...') indicates that the Tribunal can substitute its own view for the Commissioner's as to how the discretion ought to have been exercised, even where it does not consider that the Commissioner acted unreasonably. Likewise, it is suggested that a general power to review findings of fact entitles the Tribunal to substitute its own view of the facts, even in cases where there was material which was reasonably capable of supporting the Commissioner's view of the facts.

Appeals from decision of Tribunal

5.40 Any party to an appeal to the Tribunal may appeal to the court on a point of law from the decision of the Tribunal (see s 59). The appeal is to the High Court of Justice in England (if the address of the public authority is in England or Wales), the Court of Session (if its address is in Scotland) or the High Court of Justice in Northern Ireland (if its address is in Northern Ireland).

Appeals against national security certificate

5.41 There are special provisions under FOIA 2000, s 60 relating to appeals in cases where a certificate has been issued under s 23(2) or s 24(3) (matters relating to national security).[1] A certificate under s 23(2) is to the effect that certain information was directly or indirectly supplied by, or relates to, one of a number of specified bodies dealing with security information. Such information is exempt information. A certificate under s 24(3) is to the effect that certain information, not falling within s 23, is required for the purpose of safeguarding national security. Such information is also exempt information. Section 23 (though not s 24) confers absolute exemption (see s 2(3)).[2]

[1]   As to ss 23 and 24, see paras 4.24–4.38.
[2]   As to s 2, see para 4.4 et seq.

5.42   Under s 60(1), both the Commissioner and any applicant whose request for information is affected by the issue of the certificate may appeal to the Tribunal against it. There is a significant difference between the Tribunal's powers in relation to a certificate under s 23(2) and under s 24(3).

5.43   In relation to a certificate under s 23(2), the Tribunal may quash the certificate if it finds that the information referred to in the certificate was not exempt information by virtue of s 23(1). The question under s 23(1) is whether particular information was either supplied by (whether directly or indirectly), or relates to, certain bodies dealing with security matters. The Tribunal is entitled to substitute its own view on that question for the view taken by the Minister signing the certificate under s 23(2). If it considers that the Minister took the wrong view, then the Tribunal may quash the certificate (see s 60(2)).

5.44   In relation to a certificate under s 24(3), the Tribunal may quash the certificate if, and only if, applying the principles applied by the court on an application for judicial review it finds that the Minister did not have reasonable grounds for issuing the certificate (see s 60(3)). Hence the judgment as to whether or not an exemption is required for the purpose of safeguarding national security is primarily for the Minister, not the Tribunal.

5.45   What if a ministerial certificate under s 24(3) identifies information by means of a general description, and a public authority claims in any proceedings under FOIA 2000 that particular information falls within that general description? Any other party to the proceedings may appeal to the Tribunal under s 60(4). The Tribunal may determine that the certificate does not so apply (s 60(5)), but in the absence of such a determination then the certificate shall be presumed so to apply (see s 60(4)).

5.46   The effect of s 60(4) is that, if there is a dispute between a person applying for information and a public authority as to whether information falls within the scope of a general description in a certificate issued under s 24(3), that dispute cannot be resolved by the Commissioner. The Commissioner must accept the public authority's claim that the relevant information falls within the certificate. If the person seeking the information wishes to challenge that claim then he must do so by appealing to the Tribunal.

Appeal proceedings

5.47 Procedure before the Tribunal is governed by the Data Protection Act 1998, Sch 6, as amended by FOIA 2000, Sch 4 (see s 61).

6 Miscellaneous and supplementary topics

HISTORICAL AND PUBLIC RECORDS

6.1 FOIA 2000, Pt VI (ss 62–67) contains provisions relating to historical records generally, and also relating to historical records in public record offices. The effect of these provisions is to disapply some of the exemptions in FOIA 2000, Pt II. The draft code issued by the Lord Chancellor under FOIA 2000, s 46[1] provides a framework for the management of records of public authorities and bodies subject to the Public Records Act 1958 and the Public Records Act (Northern Ireland) 1923 (see Pt I of the draft code). It also deals with the transfer and review of public records (see Pt II of the draft code).

---

[1] See Appendix 2.

6.2 Part VI begins with a definition of a 'historical record'. A record becomes a historical record at the end of the period of 30 years beginning with the year following that in which it was created (s 62(1)). Section 62(2) adds an interesting twist. Where records created at different dates are kept together in one file or other assembly for administrative purposes, all those records are to be treated as having been created when the latest of those records was created. The effect of this is that the date at which a particular document becomes a historical record can be deferred if it is filed with more recent documents. It is very difficult to see how s 62(2) is to be applied to computer records. Would, for instance, documents on the hard disk of a computer be treated as documents kept together in the same assembly?

Removal of exemptions

Historical records generally

6.3 Under s 63(1), certain FOIA 2000, Pt II exemptions are disapplied in relation to historical records. The effect, therefore, is to extend the scope of the right of access contained in s 1 in these cases. In relation to a historical record, the duty to confirm or deny (under s 1(1)(a)) and the duty to communicate (under s 1(1)(b)) are not excluded by any of the following exemptions—

- — s 28 (relations between UK administrations);
- — s 30(1) (criminal investigations and proceedings conducted by public authorities);
- — s 32 (court records);
- — s 33 (audit functions);
- — s 35 (formulation of government policy);
- — s 36 (prejudice to effective conduct of public affairs);
- — s 37(1)(a) (communications with Her Majesty or with other members of the Royal family or with the Royal household);
- — s 42 (legal professional privilege);
- — s 43 (commercial interests).[1]

---

[1] These exemptions, and those discussed in paras 6.4 and 6.5, are considered in detail in Ch 4; see para 4.15 et seq.

6.4   Section 63 also disapplies two other exemptions in FOIA 2000, Pt II after a period longer than 30 years. Section 37(1)(b) (the exemption relating to information about the conferring by the Crown of any honour or dignity) is disapplied after the end of the period of 60 years beginning with the year following that in which the record containing the information was created (s 63(3)). Section 31 (relating to law enforcement) is disapplied after the end of a period of 100 years, again beginning with the year following that in which the relevant record was created (s 63(4) and (5)).

Historical records in public record offices

6.5   There are further exemptions in relation to information contained in historical records held in public record offices, ie, in the Public Record Office and the Public Record Office of Northern Ireland (see s 64). In relation to this information, the exemptions in s 21 (information accessible by other means) and s 22 (information intended for future publication) do not apply. The exemption in s 23(1) (information relating to security bodies) does apply, but it operates as a non-absolute exemption.

6.6   There are provisions determining whether decisions in relation to public records should be taken by the records authority in question, or by the public body that transferred the information to the records authority (see ss 15, 65 and 66).[1]

---

[1] See paras 3.57–3.59.

THE AARHUS CONVENTION

6.7   The Convention on access to information, public participation in decision-making and access to justice in environmental matters (the 'Aarhus Convention') was signed at Aarhus on 25 June 1998 (see s 74(1)).

6.8   Section 74(2) designates certain parts of the Aarhus Convention as 'the information provisions', ie, Article 4, together with Articles 3 and 9 so far as relating to Article 4. Section 74(3) empowers the Secretary of State to make regulations for the purpose of implementing the information provisions of the Convention.[1]

---

[1]   The exemption in relation to environmental information is discussed at paras 4.75, 4.76.

EXISTING ENACTMENTS

6.9   Section 75 confers a power on the Secretary of State to repeal or amend, by order, any enactment which appears to him to be capable, by virtue of FOIA 2000, s 44(1)(a), of preventing the disclosure of information under s 1. Section 44(1)(a) creates an absolute exemption in relation to information, the disclosure of which is prohibited by or under any enactment.[1]

---

[1]   See para 4.90.

DISCLOSURE OF INFORMATION BETWEEN COMMISSIONER AND OMBUDSMEN

6.10   Under FOIA 2000, s 76(1), the Commissioner has the power to disclose to one of a number of Ombudsmen any information obtained by him, or furnished to him, under, or for the purposes of, FIA 2000 or the Data Protection Act 1998. The power to disclose arises where it appears to the Commissioner that the information could be the subject of an investigation by that Ombudsman under an enactment specified in s 76(1). A table in s 76(1) sets out the relevant Ombudsmen, and the relevant legislation.

6.11 Schedule 7 to the Act (as introduced by s 76(2)) contains further detailed provision relating to information disclosed by the Commissioner to the specified Ombudsmen. This takes the form of amendments to other legislation. Schedule 7 also contains amendments empowering certain Ombudsmen[1] to disclose to the Commissioner information relating to matters in respect of which the Commissioner could exercise his powers under FOIA 2000, Pts IV, V, or under s 48, or information relating to the commission of offences under s 77, or under certain provisions of the Data Protection Act 1998.

---

[1] Schedule 7 makes no provision for the three Scottish Ombudsmen to disclose information to the Commissioner. Any amendments to legislation relating to the Scottish Ombudsmen are a matter for the Scottish Parliament.

OFFENCE OF ALTERING, ETC, DISCLOSABLE RECORDS

6.12 Section 77(1) creates an offence of altering, etc, records with intent to prevent disclosure. Where a request for information has been made to a public authority under FOIA 2000, and the applicant would have been entitled (subject to the payment of any fee) to the communication of any information under s 1 or under the Data Protection Act 1998, s 7, it is an offence for any person to whom the section applies to alter, deface, block, erase, destroy or conceal any record held by the public authority with the intention of preventing disclosure of part or all of the information.

6.13 Section 77(1) applies both to the public authority and to any person who is employed by, or who is an officer of, the authority, or is subject to its direction (s 77(2)). A government department is not liable to prosecution under FOIA 2000 (s 81(3)). However, s 77 applies to a person in the public service of the Crown or to a person acting on behalf of either House of Parliament or of the Northern Ireland Assembly, in the same way as it applies to any other person (s 81(3) and (4)).

6.14 Note that the offence created by s 77(1) only applies where there has been a request for information. There is no equivalent offence where the alteration, etc, of records takes place in advance of any request for access to those records under FOIA 2000.

EXISTING POWERS

6.15 Section 78 provides that nothing in FOIA 2000 is to be taken to limit the powers of a public authority to disclose information held by it.

DEFAMATION

6.16   Section 79 provides that, where information communicated by a public authority to an applicant under FOIA 2000, s 1 was supplied to the public authority by a third person, the publication is privileged for the purpose of the law of defamation unless shown to have been made with malice. Note that this privilege does not extend to defamatory material created by the public authority itself.

COMMENCEMENT

6.17   Some parts of FOIA 2000 are already in force. Under s 87(1) certain provisions came into force on the day the Act was passed (30 November 2000), and, under s 87(2), further provisions came into force on 31 January 2001. Other minor provisions have been brought into force by the Freedom of Information Act 2000 (Commencement No 1) Order 2001.[1] However, the bulk of FOIA 2000 is not yet in force; in particular, the duties under s 1, which are the most fundamental part of the Act, have not yet come into operation.

---

[1]   SI 2001/1637 (made on 30 April 2001) brought the following provisions into force on 14 May 2001: s 18(2), (3), (5), (6), (7); Sch 2, paras 1(2), 3(2), 5, 8(1), 9(1), 11, 12, 13(3), 14(b), 15(3), 16 (and s 18(4) so far as relating to those provisions); Sch 4, paras 1, 4 (and s 61 so far as relating to those provisions); Sch 6, paras 1, 6, 7 (and s 73 so far as relating to those provisions).

6.18   Under s 87(3), all of FOIA 2000 must come into force by 30 November 2005 at the latest. However, the Lord Chancellor has already stated that it will, in fact, be fully implemented by January 2005.[1]

---

[1]   See para 1.4 for the government's timetable for bringing FOIA 2000 into force.

7 Relationship with other legislation

HUMAN RIGHTS ACT 1998

7.1 The majority of the Human Rights Act 1998 (HRA 1998) came into force on 2 October 2000,[1] and gives further effect in domestic law to the European Convention on Human Rights (the ECHR). In introducing the second reading of the FOI Bill in the House of Commons the Home Secretary (Mr Jack Straw) recognised that the Bill and the HRA 1998 were interrelated. He stated—

> 'The 1998 Act sets out the European convention's statement of basic rights. Some of those rights are absolute—such as that provided in article 3, guaranteeing freedom from torture or degrading treatment. The rights with which we have had to wrestle in the Freedom of Information Bill are not absolutes, but have to be balanced one with another. Article 10 gives a right to freedom of expression, but that has to be set against article 8 on the right to respect for a private life.
>
> We have therefore sought in the Bill to secure a balance between the right to information needed for the proper exercise of the freedom of expression and the—directly conflicting—right of individuals to protection of information about themselves; the rights that institutions, including commercial companies, should have to proper confidentiality; and the need for any organisation, including the Government, to be able to formulate its collective policies in private.'[2]

---

[1] By virtue of s 20(2) of that Act, ss 18, 20, 21(5) came into force on the date the Act was passed (9 November 1998), and s 19 was brought into force on 24 November 1998 by the Human Rights Act 1998 (Commencement) Order 1998, SI 1998/2882. The remaining provisions of the Act were brought into force on 2 October 2000 by the Human Rights Act 1998 (Commencement No 2) Order 2000, SI 2000/1851.

[2] HC 2R, 7 December 1999, col 719, 720.

7.2 Under HRA 1998, s 6, public authorities must not act inconsistently with the rights set out in the ECHR. It is likely that all of the bodies that are subject to the duties imposed by FOIA 2000, s 1 will fall within

HRA 1998, s 6. In addition, the bodies that are responsible for enforcing FOIA 2000—such as the Commissioner and the Tribunal—will come within HRA 1998, s 6.

7.3   HRA 1998, s 3 provides that, in so far as it is possible to do so, the courts must construe legislation in a way which is compatible with the ECHR.

7.4   As far as the relationship between FOIA 2000 and HRA 1998 is concerned, the most important question is this: when, if ever, does the ECHR require disclosure of information by public bodies? If disclosure is required under the ECHR, then a failure to disclose will be a breach of HRA 1998, s 6, and any tribunal or court will be obliged, if possible, to construe FOIA 2000 as requiring disclosure. There may also be questions as to whether the ECHR *prohibits* the disclosure of information. For instance, where A is seeking disclosure of personal information about B, when, if ever, will it be a breach of the ECHR for a public authority to grant such disclosure to A?

7.5   There is no general right under the ECHR of disclosure of information. However, there are a number of provisions of the ECHR that may be relevant to issues under FOIA 2000.

7.6   It is well established that Article 10 of the ECHR (freedom of expression) does not impose any obligation to disclose information which an authority does not wish to disclose. The Strasbourg court has not been receptive to the argument that Article 10 protects *access* to information on which to base an opinion, or otherwise exercise Article 10 freedom of expression more effectively. The general duty on the state under Article 10 is not to obstruct access to such information as is available.[1]

------

[1]   See *Leandler v Sweden* (1987) 9 EHRR 433; *Gaskin v United Kingdom* (1989) 12 EHRR 36.

7.7   Article 8 (respect for private and family life) provides for a right of access to information in limited circumstances. In *Gaskin*, the court held that a person who has been in the care of a public authority has the right to obtain information about his or her treatment while in care. In *Z v Finland*[1] the Court placed significant emphasis on the particular position of persons infected with HIV and on the need for careful scrutiny of any measure compelling communication or disclosure of their status. The case concerned criminal proceedings and disclosure of a witness's medical status. The court accepted that disclosure of a person's HIV status could be a prima facie interference with that person's rights under Article 8(1), requiring justification under Article 8(2). In *McMichael v United Kingdom*[2] the applicants complained that the decision-making process determining custody and

access arrangements with regard to their son did not afford the protection of their interests under Article 8. The court uph ......
complaint.

[1]   (1998) 25 EHRR 371.
[2]   (1995) 20 EHRR 205.

7.8   Other Articles of the ECHR may also be relevant to issues arising under FOIA 2000. For instance, Article 6 (right to a fair trial) may be relevant in cases where disclosure of information under FOIA 2000 is necessary in order for there to be a fair trial.

DATA PROTECTION ACT 1998

7.9   The Data Protection Act 1998 (DPA 1998) largely came into force on 1 March 2000,[1] replacing the Data Protection Act 1984. A detailed consideration of the provisions of DPA 1998, which are extremely complex, is outside the scope of this book. In broad terms, DPA 1998 imposes obligations on data controllers in relation to 'personal data'; this covers certain kinds of data that relate to identifiable living individuals. Data controllers are obliged to comply with eight data protection principles in processing personal data (see DPA 1998, s 4, Sch 1, Pt I). Data subjects enjoy various rights under DPA 1998, s 7, including a right of access to personal data.

[1]   Certain provisions came into force on the date the Act was passed (16 July 1998) by virtue of s 75(2). However, most of the Act was brought into force on 1 March 2000 by the Data Protection Act 1998 (Commencement) Order 2000, SI 2000/183.

7.10 FOIA 2000 amends the definition of data in DPA 1998, s 1, so as to ensure that it extends to all recorded information held by public authorities (see FOIA 2000, s 68(1), (2) which inserts a new DPA 1998, s 1(1)(e)). The purpose of the amendment is to ensure that DPA 1998 continues to be the main Act that governs the right of access to personal information which is held by public authorities. If the amendment had not been made, the right of access to such information would have been governed partly by DPA 1998 and partly by FOIA 2000, depending on the form in which the information was stored.

7.11 Where an application for access to personal data is made by the data subject, FOIA 2000, s 40(1) is intended to ensure that the application is dealt with under DPA 1998 and not under FOIA 2000. Where an application is made by B for access to personal data about A, the application is handled under FOIA 2000 rather than under DPA 1998, but with safeguards to protect the privacy of the data subject (see s 40(2)).[1]

[1]   Section 40 is considered in detail in Ch 4; see paras 4.77–4.83.

OTHER LEGISLATION

7.12   FOIA 2000, s 21(1) provides that information which is reasonably accessible to an applicant otherwise than under s 1 is exempt information.

7.13   Presumably the effect of this provision is that information is exempt if it is already covered by other statutory regimes requiring disclosure. For instance, the provisions inserted into the Local Government Act 1972 by the Local Government (Access to Information) Act 1985[1] confer a right to attend and receive papers for certain meetings of local authorities. Rights of access to local government information are also conferred by the Local Authorities (Executive Arrangements) (Access to Information) (England) Regulations 2000.[2]

[1]   The Local Government (Access to Information) Act 1985, s 1 inserts the Local Government Act 1972, ss 100A–100K and Sch 12A.
[2]   SI 2000/3272.

7.14   Other provisions giving public access to information include the Land Registration Act 1988 (giving public access to the land register), the Environmental Protection Act 1990 (giving access to various pollution registers) and the Environmental Information Regulations 1992 (giving access to a wide range of environmental information).[1]

[1]   SI 1992/3240. See also, para 4.75.

Appendix 1

Freedom of Information Act 2000

Freedom of Information Act 2000 (Commencement No 1) Order 2001, SI 2001/1637

Freedom of Information Act 2000

(2000 c 36)

ARRANGEMENT OF SECTIONS

PART I
ACCESS TO INFORMATION HELD BY PUBLIC AUTHORITIES

Right to information

PART II
EXEMPT INFORMATION

An Act to make provision for the disclosure of information held by public authorities or by persons providing services for them and to amend the Data Protection Act 1998 and the Public Records Act 1958; and for connected purposes.   *[30 November 2000]*

Parliamentary debates.
House of Commons:
2nd Reading 7 December 1999: 340 HC Official Report (6th series) col 714.
Committee Stages 21 December 1999–10 February 2000: HC Official Report, SC B (Freedom of Information Bill).
Remaining Stages 4 April 2000: 347 HC Official Report (6th series) col 830; 5 April 2000: 347 HC Official Report (6th series) col 981.
Consideration of Lords' Amendments 27 November 2000: 357 HC Official Report (6th series) col 718.
House of Lords:
2nd Reading 20 April 2000: 612 HL Official Report (5th series) col 823.
Committee Stages 17 October 2000: 617 HL Official Report (5th series) col 884; 19 October 2000: 617 HL Official Report (5th series) col 1208; 24 October 2000: 618 HL Official Report (5th series) col 273; 25 October 2000: 618 HL Official Report (5th series) col 407.
Report Stage 14 November 2000: 619 HL Official Report (5th series) col 134.
3rd Reading 22 November 2000: 619 HL Official Report (5th series) col 817.

PART I
ACCESS TO INFORMATION HELD BY PUBLIC AUTHORITIES

Right to information

1 General right of access to information held by public authorities

(1)   Any person making a request for information to a public authority is entitled—

    (a)   to be informed in writing by the public authority whether it holds information of the description specified in the request, and

    (b)   if that is the case, to have that information communicated to him.

(2)   Subsection (1) has effect subject to the following provisions of this section and to the provisions of sections 2, 9, 12 and 14.

(3)   Where a public authority—

    (a)   reasonably requires further information in order to identify and locate the information requested, and

    (b)   has informed the applicant of that requirement,

the authority is not obliged to comply with subsection (1) unless it is supplied with that further information.

(4)   The information—

    (a)   in respect of which the applicant is to be informed under subsection (1)(a), or

    (b)   which is to be communicated under subsection (1)(b),

is the information in question held at the time when the request is received, except that account may be taken of any amendment or deletion made between that time and the time when the information is to be communicated under subsection (1)(b), being an amendment or deletion that would have been made regardless of the receipt of the request.

(5)   A public authority is to be taken to have complied with subsection (1)(a) in relation to any information if it has communicated the information to the applicant in accordance with subsection (1)(b).

(6)   In this Act, the duty of a public authority to comply with subsection (1)(a) is referred to as "the duty to confirm or deny".

Definitions   For "public authority", see s 3(1); for "request for information", see s 8; for "information", see s 84.
References   See paras 2.4, 2.5, 2.17, 2.24, 2.27, 3.2, 3.3–3.7, 3.18, 3.23, 3.29, 3.30, 3.32, 3.45, 3.46, 3.48, 4.1, 4.2, 4.5, 4.7, 4.27, 4.31, 4.32, 4.71, 5.16, 5.26, 6.3, 6.9, 6.12, 6.16, 6.17.

---

2 Effect of the exemptions in Part II

(1)   Where any provision of Part II states that the duty to confirm or deny does not arise in relation to any information, the effect of the provision is that where either—

    (a)   the provision confers absolute exemption, or

    (b)   in all the circumstances of the case, the public interest in maintaining the exclusion of the duty to confirm or deny outweighs the public interest in disclosing whether the public authority holds the information,

section 1(1)(a) does not apply.

(2)   In respect of any information which is exempt information by virtue of any provision of Part II, section 1(1)(b) does not apply if or to the extent that—

    (a)   the information is exempt information by virtue of a provision conferring absolute exemption, or

    (b)   in all the circumstances of the case, the public interest in maintaining the exemption outweighs the public interest in disclosing the information.

(3)   For the purposes of this section, the following provisions of Part II (and no others) are to be regarded as conferring absolute exemption—

    (a)   section 21,

    (b)   section 23,

    (c)   section 32,

    (d)   section 34,

    (e)   section 36 so far as relating to information held by the House of Commons or the House of Lords,

    (f)   in section 40—

        (i)   subsection (1), and

        (ii)   subsection (2) so far as relating to cases where the first condition referred to in that subsection is satisfied by virtue of subsection (3)(a)(i) or (b) of that section,

    (g)   section 41, and

    (h)   section 44.

Definitions   For "the duty to confirm or deny", see s 1(6); for "public authority", see s 3(1); for "information", see s 84.
References   See paras 2.5, 2.25, 3.3, 3.23, 4.4, 4.7, 4.8, 4.10, 4.23, 4.34, 4.63, 4.70, 4.82, 4.87, 5.41.

---

3 Public authorities

(1)   In this Act "public authority" means—

    (a)   subject to section 4(4), any body which, any other person who, or the holder of any office which—

        (i)   is listed in Schedule 1, or

        (ii)   is designated by order under section 5, or

    (b)   a publicly-owned company as defined by section 6.

(2)   For the purposes of this Act, information is held by a public authority if—

    (a)   it is held by the authority, otherwise than on behalf of another person, or

    (b)   it is held by another person on behalf of the authority.

Definitions   As to "body" and for "information", see s 84.
References   See paras 3.9, 3.11.

---

4 Amendment of Schedule 1

(1)   The [Lord Chancellor] may by order amend Schedule 1 by adding to that Schedule a reference to any body or the holder of any office which (in either case) is not for the time being listed in that Schedule but as respects which both the first and the second conditions below are satisfied.

(2)   The first condition is that the body or office—

    (a)   is established by virtue of Her Majesty's prerogative or by an enactment or by subordinate legislation, or

    (b)   is established in any other way by a Minister of the Crown in his capacity as Minister, by a government department or by the National Assembly for Wales.

(3)   The second condition is—

    (a)   in the case of a body, that the body is wholly or partly constituted by appointment made by the Crown, by a Minister of the Crown, by a government department or by the National Assembly for Wales, or

    (b)   in the case of an office, that appointments to the office are made by the Crown, by a Minister of the Crown, by a government department or by the National Assembly for Wales.

(4)   If either the first or the second condition above ceases to be satisfied as respects any body or office which is listed in Part VI or VII of Schedule 1, that body or the holder of that office shall cease to be a public authority by virtue of the entry in question.

(5)   The [Lord Chancellor] may by order amend Schedule 1 by removing from Part VI or VII of that Schedule an entry relating to any body or office—

    (a)   which has ceased to exist, or

    (b)   as respects which either the first or the second condition above has ceased to be satisfied.

(6)   An order under subsection (1) may relate to a specified person or office or to persons or offices falling within a specified description.

(7)   Before making an order under subsection (1), the [Lord Chancellor] shall—

    (a)   if the order adds to Part II, III, IV or VI of Schedule 1 a reference to—

        (i)   a body whose functions are exercisable only or mainly in or as regards Wales, or

        (ii)   the holder of an office whose functions are exercisable only or mainly in or as regards Wales, consult the National Assembly for Wales, and

    (b)   if the order relates to a body which, or the holder of any office who, if the order were made, would be a Northern Ireland public authority, consult the First Minister and deputy First Minister in Northern Ireland.

(8)   This section has effect subject to section 80.

(9)   In this section "Minister of the Crown" includes a Northern Ireland Minister.

Definitions   As to "body", "enactment" and "government department" and for "Minister of the Crown", "Northern Ireland public authority" and "subordinate legislation", see s 84 (noting, as to "Minister of the crown", sub-s (6) above).
Amendments   Sub-ss (1), (5), (7): words in square brackets substituted by the Transfer of Functions (Miscellaneous) Order 2001, SI 2001/3500, art 8, Sch 2, para 8(1)(a).
References   See paras 3.9, 3.12, 3.13, 3.15.

5 Further power to designate public authorities

(1)   The [Lord Chancellor] may by order desi,gnate as a public authority for the purposes of this Act any person who is neither listed in Schedule 1 nor capable of being added to that Schedule by an order under section 4(1), but who—

    (a)   appears to the [Lord Chancellor] to exercise functions of a public nature, or

    (b)   is providing under a contract made with a public authority any service whose provision is a function of that authority.

(2)   An order under this section may designate a specified person or office or persons or offices falling within a specified description.

(3)   Before making an order under this section, the [Lord Chancellor] shall consult every person to whom the order relates, or persons appearing to him to represent such persons.

(4)   This section has effect subject to section 80.

Definitions   For "public authority", see s 3(1).
Amendments   Sub-ss (1), (3),: words in square brackets substituted by the Transfer of Functions (Miscellaneous) Order 2001, SI 2001/3500, art 8, Sch 2, para 8(1)(b).
References   See paras 3.9, 3.13, 3.15, 4.83.

6 Publicly-owned companies

(1)   A company is a "publicly-owned company" for the purposes of section 3(1)(b) if—

    (a)   it is wholly owned by the Crown, or

    (b)   it is wholly owned by any public authority listed in Schedule 1 other than—

        (i)   a government department, or

        (ii)   any authority which is listed only in relation to particular information.

(2)   For the purposes of this section—

    (a)   a company is wholly owned by the Crown if it has no members except—

        (i)   Ministers of the Crown, government departments or companies wholly owned by the Crown, or

        (ii)   persons acting on behalf of Ministers of the Crown, government departments or companies wholly owned by the Crown, and

    (b)   a company is wholly owned by a public authority other than a government department if it has no members except—

        (i)   that public authority or companies wholly owned by that public authority, or

        (ii)   persons acting on behalf of that public authority or of companies wholly owned by that public authority.

(3)   In this section—

    "company" includes any body corporate;

    "Minister of the Crown" includes a Northern Ireland Minister.

Definitions   For "public authority", see s 3(1); as to "government department" and for "information", "Ministers of the Crown" and "Northern Ireland Minister", see s 84.
References   See paras 3.9, 3.14.

7 Public authorities to which Act has limited application

(1)   Where a public authority is listed in Schedule 1 only in relation to information of a specified description, nothing in Parts I to V of this Act applies to any other information held by the authority.

(2)   An order under section 4(1) may, in adding an entry to Schedule 1, list the public authority only in relation to information of a specified description.

(3)   The [Lord Chancellor] may by order amend Schedule 1—
    (a)   by limiting to information of a specified description the entry relating to any public authority, or
    (b)   by removing or amending any limitation to information of a specified description which is for the time being contained in any entry.

(4)   Before making an order under subsection (3), the [Lord Chancellor] shall—
    (a)   if the order relates to the National Assembly for Wales or a Welsh public authority, consult the National Assembly for Wales,
    (b)   if the order relates to the Northern Ireland Assembly, consult the Presiding Officer of that Assembly, and
    (c)   if the order relates to a Northern Ireland department or a Northern Ireland public authority, consult the First Minister and deputy First Minister in Northern Ireland.

(5)   An order under section 5(1)(a) must specify the functions of the public authority designated by the order with respect to which the designation is to have effect; and nothing in Parts I to V of this Act applies to information which is held by the authority but does not relate to the exercise of those functions.

(6)   An order under section 5(1)(b) must specify the services provided under contract with respect to which the designation is to have effect; and nothing in Parts I to V of this Act applies to information which is held by the public authority designated by the order but does not relate to the provision of those services.

(7)   Nothing in Parts I to V of this Act applies in relation to any information held by a publicly-owned company which is excluded information in relation to that company.

(8)   In subsection (7) "excluded information", in relation to a publicly-owned company, means information which is of a description specified in relation to that company in an order made by the [Lord Chancellor] for the purposes of this subsection.

(9)   In this section "publicly-owned company" has the meaning given by section 6.

Definitions   For "public authority", see s 3(1); for "information", see s 84.
Amendments   Sub-ss (3), (4), (8): words in square brackets substituted by the Transfer of Functions (Miscellaneous) Order 2001, SI 2001/3500, art 8, Sch 2, para 8(1)(c).
References   See paras 3.9, 3.15.

8 Request for information

(1)   In this Act any reference to a "request for information" is a reference to such a request which—
    (a)   is in writing,

(b)   states the name of the applicant and an address for correspondence, and

(c)   describes the information requested.

(2)   For the purposes of subsection (1)(a), a request is to be treated as made in writing where the text of the request—

(a)   is transmitted by electronic means,

(b)   is received in legible form, and

(c)   is capable of being used for subsequent reference.

Definitions   For "applicant" and "information", see s 84.
References   See paras 2.15, 2.16, 3.16.

---

9 Fees

(1)   A public authority to whom a request for information is made may, within the period for complying with section 1(1), give the applicant a notice in writing (in this Act referred to as a "fees notice") stating that a fee of an amount specified in the notice is to be charged by the authority for complying with section 1(1).

(2)   Where a fees notice has been given to the applicant, the public authority is not obliged to comply with section 1(1) unless the fee is paid within the period of three months beginning with the day on which the fees notice is given to the applicant.

(3)   Subject to subsection (5), any fee under this section must be determined by the public authority in accordance with regulations made by the [Lord Chancellor].

(4)   Regulations under subsection (3) may, in particular, provide—

(a)   that no fee is to be payable in prescribed cases,

(b)   that any fee is not to exceed such maximum as may be specified in, or determined in accordance with, the regulations, and

(c)   that any fee is to be calculated in such manner as may be prescribed by the regulations.

(5)   Subsection (3) does not apply where provision is made by or under any enactment as to the fee that may be charged by the public authority for the disclosure of the information.

Definitions   For "public authority", see s 3(1); for "request for information", see s 8; for "applicant" and as to "enactment" and for "information" and "prescribed", see s 84.
Amendments   Sub-s (3): words in square brackets substituted by the Transfer of Functions (Miscellaneous) Order 2001, SI 2001/3500, art 8, Sch 2, para 8(1)(d).
References   See paras 2.21, 2.24, 3.3, 3.22, 3.29, 3.30, 3.32, 4.2.

---

10 Time for compliance with request

(1)   Subject to subsections (2) and (3), a public authority must comply with section 1(1) promptly and in any event not later than the twentieth working day following the date of receipt.

(2)   Where the authority has given a fees notice to the applicant and the fee is paid in accordance with section 9(2), the working days in the period beginning with the day on which the fees notice is given to the applicant and

ending with the day on which the fee is received by the authority are to be disregarded in calculating for the purposes of subsection (1) the twentieth working day following the date of receipt.

(3)   If, and to the extent that—

    (a)   section 1(1)(a) would not apply if the condition in section 2(1)(b) were satisfied, or

    (b)   section 1(1)(b) would not apply if the condition in section 2(2)(b) were satisfied,

the public authority need not comply with section 1(1)(a) or (b) until such time as is reasonable in the circumstances; but this subsection does not affect the time by which any notice under section 17(1) must be given.

(4)   The [Lord Chancellor] may by regulations provide that subsections (1) and (2) are to have effect as if any reference to the twentieth working day following the date of receipt were a reference to such other day, not later than the sixtieth working day following the date of receipt, as may be specified in, or determined in accordance with, the regulations.

(5)   Regulations under subsection (4) may—

    (a)   prescribe different days in relation to different cases, and

    (b)   confer a discretion on the Commissioner.

(6)   In this section—

    "the date of receipt" means—

        (a)   the day on which the public authority receives the request for information, or

        (b)   if later, the day on which it receives the information referred to in section 1(3);

    "working day" means any day other than a Saturday, a Sunday, Christmas Day, Good Friday or a day which is a bank holiday under the Banking and Financial Dealings Act 1971 in any part of the United Kingdom.

Definitions   For "public authority", see s 3(1); for "request for information", see s 8; for "fees notice", see s 9(1); for "applicant", "the Commissioner", "information" and "prescribe", see s 84.
Amendments   Sub-s (4): words in square brackets substituted by the Transfer of Functions (Miscellaneous) Order 2001, SI 2001/3500, art 8, Sch 2, para 8(1)(e).
References   See paras 2.19, 2.21, 2.26, 3.21–3.25, 3.30, 3.46, 3.47, 3.49, 3.51, 4.80.

---

11 Means by which communication to be made

(1)   Where, on making his request for information, the applicant expresses a preference for communication by any one or more of the following means, namely—

    (a)   the provision to the applicant of a copy of the information in permanent form or in another form acceptable to the applicant,

    (b)   the provision to the applicant of a reasonable opportunity to inspect a record containing the information, and

    (c)   the provision to the applicant of a digest or summary of the information in permanent form or in another form acceptable to the applicant,

the public authority shall so far as reasonably practicable give effect to that preference.

(2)   In determining for the purposes of this section whether it is reasonably practicable to communicate information by particular means, the public authority may have regard to all the circumstances, including the cost of doing so.

(3)   Where the public authority determines that it is not reasonably practicable to comply with any preference expressed by the applicant in making his request, the authority shall notify the applicant of the reasons for its determination.

(4)   Subject to subsection (1), a public authority may comply with a request by communicating information by any means which are reasonable in the circumstances.

Definitions   For "public authority", see s 3(1); for "request for information", see s 8; for "applicant" and "information", see s 84.
References   See paras 2.15, 2.20, 3.26, 3.27, 5.16.

12 Exemption where cost of compliance exceeds appropriate limit

(1)   Section 1(1) does not oblige a public authority to comply with a request for information if the authority estimates that the cost of complying with the request would exceed the appropriate limit.

(2)   Subsection (1) does not exempt the public authority from its obligation to comply with paragraph (a) of section 1(1) unless the estimated cost of complying with that paragraph alone would exceed the appropriate limit.

(3)   In subsections (1) and (2) "the appropriate limit" means such amount as may be prescribed, and different amounts may be prescribed in relation to different cases.

(4)   The [Lord Chancellor] may by regulations provide that, in such circumstances as may be prescribed, where two or more requests for information are made to a public authority—

(a)   by one person, or

(b)   by different persons who appear to the public authority to be acting in concert or in pursuance of a campaign,

the estimated cost of complying with any of the requests is to be taken to be the estimated total cost of complying with all of them.

(5)   The [Lord Chancellor] may by regulations make provision for the purposes of this section as to the costs to be estimated and as to the manner in which they are to be estimated.

Definitions   For "public authority", see s 3(1); for "request for information", see s 8; for "information" and "prescribed", see s 84.
Amendments Sub-ss (4), (5): words in square brackets substituted by the Transfer of Functions (Miscellaneous) Order 2001, SI 2001/3500, art 8, Sch 2, para 8(1)(f).
References   See paras 2.6, 2.24, 3.3, 3.33–3.35, 3.40, 3.41, 3.51, 4.2.

13 Fees for disclosure where cost of compliance exceeds appropriate limit

(1)   A public authority may charge for the communication of any information whose communication—

    (a)   is not required by section 1(1) because the cost of complying with the request for information exceeds the amount which is the appropriate limit for the purposes of section 12(1) and (2), and

    (b)   is not otherwise required by law,

such fee as may be determined by the public authority in accordance with regulations made by the [Lord Chancellor].

(2)   Regulations under this section may, in particular, provide—

    (a)   that any fee is not to exceed such maximum as may be specified in, or determined in accordance with, the regulations, and

    (b)   that any fee is to be calculated in such manner as may be prescribed by the regulations.

(3)   Subsection (1) does not apply where provision is made by or under any enactment as to the fee that may be charged by the public authority for the disclosure of the information.

Definitions   For "public authority", see s 3(1); for "request for information", see s 8; for "information", see s 84.
Amendments   Sub-s (1): words in square brackets substituted by the Transfer of Functions (Miscellaneous) Order 2001, SI 2001/3500, art 8, Sch 2, para 8(1)(g).
References   See paras 3.33, 3.34.

14 Vexatious or repeated requests

(1)   Section 1(1) does not oblige a public authority to comply with a request for information if the request is vexatious.

(2)   Where a public authority has previously complied with a request for information which was made by any person, it is not obliged to comply with a subsequent identical or substantially similar request from that person unless a reasonable interval has elapsed between compliance with the previous request and the making of the current request.

Definitions   For "public authority", see s 3(1); for "request for information", see s 8; for "information", see s 84.
References   See paras 2.5–2.7, 2.24, 3.3, 3.36–3.39, 3.40, 3.42, 3.51, 4.2.

15 Special provisions relating to public records transferred to Public Record Office, etc

(1)   Where—

    (a)   the appropriate records authority receives a request for information which relates to information which is, or if it existed would be, contained in a transferred public record, and

    (b)   either of the conditions in subsection (2) is satisfied in relation to any of that information,

that authority shall, within the period for complying with section 1(1), send a copy of the request to the responsible authority.

(2)   The conditions referred to in subsection (1)(b) are—

    (a)   that the duty to confirm or deny is expressed to be excluded only by a provision of Part II not specified in subsection (3) of section 2, and

    (b)   that the information is exempt information only by virtue of a provision of Part II not specified in that subsection.

(3)   On receiving the copy, the responsible authority shall, within such time as is reasonable in all the circumstances, inform the appropriate records authority of the determination required by virtue of subsection (3) or (4) of section 66.

(4)   In this Act "transferred public record" means a public record which has been transferred—

(a)   to the Public Record Office,

(b)   to another place of deposit appointed by the Lord Chancellor under the Public Records Act 1958, or

(c)   to the Public Record Office of Northern Ireland.

(5)   In this Act—

"appropriate records authority", in relation to a transferred public record, means—

(a)   in a case falling within subsection (4)(a), the Public Record Office,

(b)   in a case falling within subsection (4)(b), the Lord Chancellor, and

(c)   in a case falling within subsection (4)(c), the Public Record Office of Northern Ireland;

"responsible authority", in relation to a transferred public record, means—

(a)   in the case of a record transferred as mentioned in subsection (4)(a) or (b) from a government department in the charge of a Minister of the Crown, the Minister of the Crown who appears to the Lord Chancellor to be primarily concerned,

(b)   in the case of a record transferred as mentioned in subsection (4)(a) or (b) from any other person, the person who appears to the Lord Chancellor to be primarily concerned,

(c)   in the case of a record transferred to the Public Record Office of Northern Ireland from a government department in the charge of a Minister of the Crown, the Minister of the Crown who appears to the appropriate Northern Ireland Minister to be primarily concerned,

(d)   in the case of a record transferred to the Public Record Office of Northern Ireland from a Northern Ireland department, the Northern Ireland Minister who appears to the appropriate Northern Ireland Minister to be primarily concerned, or

(e)   in the case of a record transferred to the Public Record Office of Northern Ireland from any other person, the person who appears to the appropriate Northern Ireland Minister to be primarily concerned.

Definitions   For "the duty to confirm or deny", see s 1(6); for "public authority", see s 3(1); for "request for information", see s 8; for "applicant", "government department", "Minister of the Crown", "Northern Ireland Minister" and "information", see s 84.
References   See paras 3.57, 3.58, 6.6.

16 Duty to provide advice and assistance

(1)   It shall be the duty of a public authority to provide advice and assistance, so far as it would be reasonable to expect the authority to do so, to persons who propose to make, or have made, requests for information to it.

(2)   Any public authority which, in relation to the provision of advice or assistance in any case, conforms with the code of practice under section 45 is to be taken to comply with the duty imposed by subsection (1) in relation to that case.

Definitions   For "public authority", see s 3(1); for "request for information", see s 8; for "information", see s 84.
References   See paras 2.18, 3.19, 3.20.

Refusal of request

17 Refusal of request

(1)   A public authority which, in relation to any request for information, is to any extent relying on a claim that any provision of Part II relating to the duty to confirm or deny is relevant to the request or on a claim that information is exempt information must, within the time for complying with section 1(1), give the applicant a notice which—

(a)   states that fact,

(b)   specifies the exemption in question, and

(c)   states (if that would not otherwise be apparent) why the exemption applies.

(2)   Where—

(a)   in relation to any request for information, a public authority is, as respects any information, relying on a claim—

(i)   that any provision of Part II which relates to the duty to confirm or deny and is not specified in section 2(3) is relevant to the request, or

(ii)   that the information is exempt information only by virtue of a provision not specified in section 2(3), and

(b)   at the time when the notice under subsection (1) is given to the applicant, the public authority (or, in a case falling within section 66(3) or (4), the responsible authority) has not yet reached a decision as to the application of subsection (1)(b) or (2)(b) of section 2,

the notice under subsection (1) must indicate that no decision as to the application of that provision has yet been reached and must contain an estimate of the date by which the authority expects that such a decision will have been reached.

(3)   A public authority which, in relation to any request for information, is to any extent relying on a claim that subsection (1)(b) or (2)(b) of section 2 applies must, either in the notice under subsection (1) or in a separate notice given within such time as is reasonable in the circumstances, state the reasons for claiming—

(a)   that, in all the circumstances of the case, the public interest in maintaining the exclusion of the duty to confirm or deny outweighs the public interest in disclosing whether the authority holds the information, or

(b)   that, in all the circumstances of the case, the public interest in maintaining the exemption outweighs the public interest in disclosing the information.

(4)   A public authority is not obliged to make a statement under subsection (1)(c) or (3) if, or to the extent that, the statement would involve the disclosure of information which would itself be exempt information.

(5)   A public authority which, in relation to any request for information, is relying on a claim that section 12 or 14 applies must, within the time for complying with section 1(1), give the applicant a notice stating that fact.

(6)   Subsection (5) does not apply where—
- (a)   the public authority is relying on a claim that section 14 applies,
- (b)   the authority has given the applicant a notice, in relation to a previous request for information, stating that it is relying on such a claim, and
- (c)   it would in all the circumstances be unreasonable to expect the authority to serve a further notice under subsection (5) in relation to the current request.

(7)   A notice under subsection (1), (3) or (5) must—
- (a)   contain particulars of any procedure provided by the public authority for dealing with complaints about the handling of requests for information or state that the authority does not provide such a procedure, and
- (b)   contain particulars of the right conferred by section 50.

Definitions   For "the duty to confirm or deny", see s 1(6); for "public authority", see s 3(1); for "request for information", see s 8; for "applicant", "exempt information" and "information", see s 84.
References   See paras 3.23, 3.44–3.51, 5.16.

The Information Commissioner and the Information Tribunal

18 The Information Commissioner and the Information Tribunal

(1)   The Data Protection Commissioner shall be known instead as the Information Commissioner.

(2)   The Data Protection Tribunal shall be known instead as the Information Tribunal.

(3)   In this Act—
- (a)   the Information Commissioner is referred to as "the Commissioner", and
- (b)   the Information Tribunal is referred to as "the Tribunal".

(4)   Schedule 2 (which makes provision consequential on subsections (1) and (2) and amendments of the Data Protection Act 1998 relating to the extension by this Act of the functions of the Commissioner and the Tribunal) has effect.

(5)   If the person who held office as Data Protection Commissioner immediately before the day on which this Act is passed remains in office as Information Commissioner at the end of the period of two years beginning with that day, he shall vacate his office at the end of that period.

(6)   Subsection (5) does not prevent the re-appointment of a person whose appointment is terminated by that subsection.

(7)   In the application of paragraph 2(4)(b) and (5) of Schedule 5 to the Data Protection Act 1998 (Commissioner not to serve for more than fifteen years and not to be appointed, except in special circumstances, for a third or subsequent term) to anything done after the passing of this Act, there shall be left out of account any term of office served by virtue of an appointment made before the passing of this Act.

References   See paras 3.52, 5.35.

Publication schemes

19 Publication schemes

(1)   It shall be the duty of every public authority—
  (a)   to adopt and maintain a scheme which relates to the publication of information by the authority and is approved by the Commissioner (in this Act referred to as a "publication scheme"),
  (b)   to publish information in accordance with its publication scheme, and
  (c)   from time to time to review its publication scheme.

(2)   A publication scheme must—
  (a)   specify classes of information which the public authority publishes or intends to publish,
  (b)   specify the manner in which information of each class is, or is intended to be, published, and
  (c)   specify whether the material is, or is intended to be, available to the public free of charge or on payment.

(3)   In adopting or reviewing a publication scheme, a public authority shall have regard to the public interest—
  (a)   in allowing public access to information held by the authority, and
  (b)   in the publication of reasons for decisions made by the authority.

(4)   A public authority shall publish its publication scheme in such manner as it thinks fit.

(5)   The Commissioner may, when approving a scheme, provide that his approval is to expire at the end of a specified period.

(6)   Where the Commissioner has approved the publication scheme of any public authority, he may at any time give notice to the public authority revoking his approval of the scheme as from the end of the period of six months beginning with the day on which the notice is given.

(7)   Where the Commissioner—
  (a)   refuses to approve a proposed publication scheme, or
  (b)   revokes his approval of a publication scheme,
he must give the public authority a statement of his reasons for doing so.

Definitions   For "public authority", see s 3(1); for "the Commissioner" and "information", see s 84.
References   See paras 3.54, 3.55.

20 Model publication schemes

(1)   The Commissioner may from time to time approve, in relation to public authorities falling within particular classes, model publication schemes prepared by him or by other persons.

(2)   Where a public authority falling within the class to which an approved model scheme relates adopts such a scheme without modification, no further approval of the Commissioner is required so long as the model scheme remains approved; and where such an authority adopts such a scheme with modifications, the approval of the Commissioner is required only in relation to the modifications.

(3)   The Commissioner may, when approving a model publication scheme, provide that his approval is to expire at the end of a specified period.

(4)   Where the Commissioner has approved a model publication scheme, he may at any time publish, in such manner as he thinks fit, a notice revoking his approval of the scheme as from the end of the period of six months beginning with the day on which the notice is published.

(5)   Where the Commissioner refuses to approve a proposed model publication scheme on the application of any person, he must give the person who applied for approval of the scheme a statement of the reasons for his refusal.

(6)   Where the Commissioner refuses to approve any modifications under subsection (2), he must give the public authority a statement of the reasons for his refusal.

(7)   Where the Commissioner revokes his approval of a model publication scheme, he must include in the notice under subsection (4) a statement of his reasons for doing so.

Definitions   For "public authority", see s 3(1); for "publication scheme", see s 19; for "the Commissioner", see s 84.
References   See para 3.56.

PART II
EXEMPT INFORMATION

21 Information accessible to applicant by other means

(1)   Information which is reasonably accessible to the applicant otherwise than under section 1 is exempt information.

(2)   For the purposes of subsection (1)—
   (a)   information may be reasonably accessible to the applicant even though it is accessible only on payment, and
   (b)   information is to be taken to be reasonably accessible to the applicant if it is information which the public authority or any other person is obliged by or under any enactment to communicate (otherwise than by making the information available for inspection) to members of the public on request, whether free of charge or on payment.

(3)   For the purposes of subsection (1), information which is held by a public authority and does not fall within subsection (2)(b) is not to be regarded as reasonably accessible to the applicant merely because the information is

available from the public authority itself on request, unless the information is made available in accordance with the authority's publication scheme and any payment required is specified in, or determined in accordance with, the scheme.

Definitions   For "public authority", see s 3(1); for "publication scheme", see s 19; as to "applicant" and "enactment" and for "information", see s 84.
References   See paras 2.5, 4.5, 4.19, 6.5.

22 Information intended for future publication

(1)   Information is exempt information if—

- (a)   the information is held by the public authority with a view to its publication, by the authority or any other person, at some future date (whether determined or not),
- (b)   the information was already held with a view to such publication at the time when the request for information was made, and
- (c)   it is reasonable in all the circumstances that the information should be withheld from disclosure until the date referred to in paragraph (a).

(2)   The duty to confirm or deny does not arise if, or to the extent that, compliance with section 1(1)(a) would involve the disclosure of any information (whether or not already recorded) which falls within subsection (1).

Definitions   For "the duty to confirm or deny", see s 1(6); for "public authority", see s 3(1); for "request for information", see s 8; for "information", see s 84.
References   See paras 2.5, 4.20–4.23, 6.5.

23 Information supplied by, or relating to, bodies dealing with security matters

(1)   Information held by a public authority is exempt information if it was directly or indirectly supplied to the public authority by, or relates to, any of the bodies specified in subsection (3).

(2)   A certificate signed by a Minister of the Crown certifying that the information to which it applies was directly or indirectly supplied by, or relates to, any of the bodies specified in subsection (3) shall, subject to section 60, be conclusive evidence of that fact.

(3)   The bodies referred to in subsections (1) and (2) are—

- (a)   the Security Service,
- (b)   the Secret Intelligence Service,
- (c)   the Government Communications Headquarters,
- (d)   the special forces,
- (e)   the Tribunal established under section 65 of the Regulation of Investigatory Powers Act 2000,
- (f)   the Tribunal established under section 7 of the Interception of Communications Act 1985,
- (g)   the Tribunal established under section 5 of the Security Service Act 1989,

(h) the Tribunal established under section 9 of the Intelligence Services Act 1994,

(i) the Security Vetting Appeals Panel,

(j) the Security Commission,

(k) the National Criminal Intelligence Service, and

(l) the Service Authority for the National Criminal Intelligence Service.

(4) In subsection (3)(c) "the Government Communications Headquarters" includes any unit or part of a unit of the armed forces of the Crown which is for the time being required by the Secretary of State to assist the Government Communications Headquarters in carrying out its functions.

(5) The duty to confirm or deny does not arise if, or to the extent that, compliance with section 1(1)(a) would involve the disclosure of any information (whether or not already recorded) which was directly or indirectly supplied to the public authority by, or relates to, any of the bodies specified in subsection (3).

Definitions   For "the duty to confirm or deny", see s 1(6); for "public authority", see s 3(1); for "information", "Minister of the Crown" and "the special forces", see s 84.
References   See paras 2.5, 4.24, 4.25, 4.27–4.34, 4.58, 5.41–5.43, 6.5.

---

24 National security

(1) Information which does not fall within section 23(1) is exempt information if exemption from section 1(1)(b) is required for the purpose of safeguarding national security.

(2) The duty to confirm or deny does not arise if, or to the extent that, exemption from section 1(1)(a) is required for the purpose of safeguarding national security.

(3) A certificate signed by a Minister of the Crown certifying that exemption from section 1(1)(b), or from section 1(1)(a) and (b), is, or at any time was, required for the purpose of safeguarding national security shall, subject to section 60, be conclusive evidence of that fact.

(4) A certificate under subsection (3) may identify the information to which it applies by means of a general description and may be expressed to have prospective effect.

Definitions   For "the duty to confirm or deny", see s 1(6); for "information" and "Minister of the Crown", see s 84.
References   See paras 2.5, 4.24, 4.31–4.35, 4.37, 4.38, 5.41, 5.42, 5.44–5.46.

---

25 Certificates under ss 23 and 24: supplementary provisions

(1) A document purporting to be a certificate under section 23(2) or 24(3) shall be received in evidence and deemed to be such a certificate unless the contrary is proved.

(2) A document which purports to be certified by or on behalf of a Minister of the Crown as a true copy of a certificate issued by that Minister under

section 23(2) or 24(3) shall in any legal proceedings be evidence (or, in Scotland, sufficient evidence) of that certificate.

(3)　The power conferred by section 23(2) or 24(3) on a Minister of the Crown shall not be exercisable except by a Minister who is a member of the Cabinet or by the Attorney General, the Advocate General for Scotland or the Attorney General for Northern Ireland.

Definitions　For "Minister of the Crown", see s 84.
References　See paras 2.5, 4.28, 4.33, 5.13.

26　Defence

(1)　Information is exempt information if its disclosure under this Act would, or would be likely to, prejudice—
> (a)　the defence of the British Islands or of any colony, or
> (b)　the capability, effectiveness or security of any relevant forces.

(2)　In subsection (1)(b) "relevant forces" means—
> (a)　the armed forces of the Crown, and
> (b)　any forces co-operating with those forces,

or any part of any of those forces.

(3)　The duty to confirm or deny does not arise if, or to the extent that, compliance with section 1(1)(a) would, or would be likely to, prejudice any of the matters mentioned in subsection (1).

Definitions　For "the duty to confirm or deny", see s 1(6); for "information", see s 84.
References　See paras 2.5, 4.39–4.42.

27　International relations

(1)　Information is exempt information if its disclosure under this Act would, or would be likely to, prejudice—
> (a)　relations between the United Kingdom and any other State,
> (b)　relations between the United Kingdom and any international organisation or international court,
> (c)　the interests of the United Kingdom abroad, or
> (d)　the promotion or protection by the United Kingdom of its interests abroad.

(2)　Information is also exempt information if it is confidential information obtained from a State other than the United Kingdom or from an international organisation or international court.

(3)　For the purposes of this section, any information obtained from a State, organisation or court is confidential at any time while the terms on which it was obtained require it to be held in confidence or while the circumstances in which it was obtained make it reasonable for the State, organisation or court to expect that it will be so held.

(4)　The duty to confirm or deny does not arise if, or to the extent that, compliance with section 1(1)(a)—
> (a)　would, or would be likely to, prejudice any of the matters mentioned in subsection (1), or

(b)   would involve the disclosure of any information (whether or not already recorded) which is confidential information obtained from a State other than the United Kingdom or from an international organisation or international court.

(5)   In this section—

"international court" means any international court which is not an international organisation and which is established—

(a)   by a resolution of an international organisation of which the United Kingdom is a member, or

(b)   by an international agreement to which the United Kingdom is a party;

"international organisation" means any international organisation whose members include any two or more States, or any organ of such an organisation;

"State" includes the government of any State and any organ of its government, and references to a State other than the United Kingdom include references to any territory outside the United Kingdom.

Definitions   For "the duty to confirm or deny", see s 1(6); for "information", see s 84.
References   See paras 2.5, 4.43.

---

28 Relations within the United Kingdom

(1)   Information is exempt information if its disclosure under this Act would, or would be likely to, prejudice relations between any administration in the United Kingdom and any other such administration.

(2)   In subsection (1) "administration in the United Kingdom" means—

(a)   the government of the United Kingdom,

(b)   the Scottish Administration,

(c)   the Executive Committee of the Northern Ireland Assembly, or

(d)   the National Assembly for Wales.

(3)   The duty to confirm or deny does not arise if, or to the extent that, compliance with section 1(1)(a) would, or would be likely to, prejudice any of the matters mentioned in subsection (1).

Definitions   For "the duty to confirm or deny", see s 1(6); for "information", see s 84.
References   See paras 2.5, 4.45, 4.46, 6.3.

---

29 The economy

(1)   Information is exempt information if its disclosure under this Act would, or would be likely to, prejudice—

(a)   the economic interests of the United Kingdom or of any part of the United Kingdom, or

(b)   the financial interests of any administration in the United Kingdom, as defined by section 28(2).

(2)   The duty to confirm or deny does not arise if, or to the extent that, compliance with section 1(1)(a) would, or would be likely to, prejudice any of the matters mentioned in subsection (1).

| **Definitions** | For "the duty to confirm or deny", see s 1(6); for "information", see s 84. |
| **References** | See paras 2.5, 4.46. |

30 Investigations and proceedings conducted by public authorities

(1)   Information held by a public authority is exempt information if it has at any time been held by the authority for the purposes of—

    (a)   any investigation which the public authority has a duty to conduct with a view to it being ascertained—

        (i)   whether a person should be charged with an offence, or

        (ii)   whether a person charged with an offence is guilty of it,

    (b)   any investigation which is conducted by the authority and in the circumstances may lead to a decision by the authority to institute criminal proceedings which the authority has power to conduct, or

    (c)   any criminal proceedings which the authority has power to conduct.

(2)   Information held by a public authority is exempt information if—

    (a)   it was obtained or recorded by the authority for the purposes of its functions relating to—

        (i)   investigations falling within subsection (1)(a) or (b),

        (ii)   criminal proceedings which the authority has power to conduct,

        (iii)   investigations (other than investigations falling within subsection (1)(a) or (b)) which are conducted by the authority for any of the purposes specified in section 31(2) and either by virtue of Her Majesty's prerogative or by virtue of powers conferred by or under any enactment, or

        (iv)   civil proceedings which are brought by or on behalf of the authority and arise out of such investigations, and

    (b)   it relates to the obtaining of information from confidential sources.

(3)   The duty to confirm or deny does not arise in relation to information which is (or if it were held by the public authority would be) exempt information by virtue of subsection (1) or (2).

(4)   In relation to the institution or conduct of criminal proceedings or the power to conduct them, references in subsection (1)(b) or (c) and subsection (2)(a) to the public authority include references—

    (a)   to any officer of the authority,

    (b)   in the case of a government department other than a Northern Ireland department, to the Minister of the Crown in charge of the department, and

    (c)   in the case of a Northern Ireland department, to the Northern Ireland Minister in charge of the department.

(5)   In this section—

"criminal proceedings" includes—

    (a)   proceedings before a court-martial constituted under the Army Act 1955, the Air Force Act 1955 or the Naval Discipline Act 1957 *or a disciplinary court constituted under section 52G of the Act of 1957,*

(b) proceedings on dealing summarily with a charge under the Army Act 1955 or the Air Force Act 1955 or on summary trial under the Naval Discipline Act 1957,

(c) proceedings before a court established by section 83ZA of the Army Act 1955, section 83ZA of the Air Force Act 1955 or section 52FF of the Naval Discipline Act 1957 (summary appeal courts),

(d) proceedings before the Courts-Martial Appeal Court, and

(e) proceedings before a Standing Civilian Court;

"offence" includes any offence under the Army Act 1955, the Air Force Act 1955 or the Naval Discipline Act 1957.

(6) In the application of this section to Scotland—

(a) in subsection (1)(b), for the words from "a decision" to the end there is substituted "a decision by the authority to make a report to the procurator fiscal for the purpose of enabling him to determine whether criminal proceedings should be instituted",

(b) in subsections (1)(c) and (2)(a)(ii) for "which the authority has power to conduct" there is substituted "which have been instituted in consequence of a report made by the authority to the procurator fiscal", and

(c) for any reference to a person being charged with an offence there is substituted a reference to the person being prosecuted for the offence.

Amendment   Sub-s (5): words in italics repealed by the Armed Forces Act 2001, s 38, Sch 7, Pt 1, as from a day to be appointed.
Definitions   For "the duty to confirm or deny", see s 1(6); for "public authority", see s 3(1); as to "enactment" and "government department" and for "information", "Minister of the Crown" and "the Northern Ireland Minister", see s 84.
References   See paras 2.5, 4.48–4.52, 6.3.

31 Law enforcement

(1)   Information which is not exempt information by virtue of section 30 is exempt information if its disclosure under this Act would, or would be likely to, prejudice—

(a) the prevention or detection of crime,

(b) the apprehension or prosecution of offenders,

(c) the administration of justice,

(d) the assessment or collection of any tax or duty or of any imposition of a similar nature,

(e) the operation of the immigration controls,

(f) the maintenance of security and good order in prisons or in other institutions where persons are lawfully detained,

(g) the exercise by any public authority of its functions for any of the purposes specified in subsection (2),

(h) any civil proceedings which are brought by or on behalf of a public authority and arise out of an investigation conducted, for any of the purposes specified in subsection (2), by or on behalf of the authority by virtue of Her Majesty's prerogative or by virtue of powers conferred by or under an enactment, or

(i) any inquiry held under the Fatal Accidents and Sudden Deaths Inquiries (Scotland) Act 1976 to the extent that the inquiry arises out of an investigation conducted, for any of the purposes specified in subsection (2), by or on behalf of the authority by virtue of Her Majesty's prerogative or by virtue of powers conferred by or under an enactment.

(2) The purposes referred to in subsection (1)(g) to (i) are—

    (a) the purpose of ascertaining whether any person has failed to comply with the law,

    (b) the purpose of ascertaining whether any person is responsible for any conduct which is improper,

    (c) the purpose of ascertaining whether circumstances which would justify regulatory action in pursuance of any enactment exist or may arise,

    (d) the purpose of ascertaining a person's fitness or competence in relation to the management of bodies corporate or in relation to any profession or other activity which he is, or seeks to become, authorised to carry on,

    (e) the purpose of ascertaining the cause of an accident,

    (f) the purpose of protecting charities against misconduct or mismanagement (whether by trustees or other persons) in their administration,

    (g) the purpose of protecting the property of charities from loss or misapplication,

    (h) the purpose of recovering the property of charities,

    (i) the purpose of securing the health, safety and welfare of persons at work, and

    (j) the purpose of protecting persons other than persons at work against risk to health or safety arising out of or in connection with the actions of persons at work.

(3) The duty to confirm or deny does not arise if, or to the extent that, compliance with section 1(1)(a) would, or would be likely to, prejudice any of the matters mentioned in subsection (1).

Definitions   For "the duty to confirm or deny", see s 1(6); for "public authority", see s 3(1); as to "enactment" and for "information", see s 84.
References   See paras 2.5, 4.50, 4.52, 6.4.

---

32 Court records, etc

(1) Information held by a public authority is exempt information if it is held only by virtue of being contained in—

    (a) any document filed with, or otherwise placed in the custody of, a court for the purposes of proceedings in a particular cause or matter,

    (b) any document served upon, or by, a public authority for the purposes of proceedings in a particular cause or matter, or

    (c) any document created by—

        (i) court, or

        (ii) a member of the administrative staff of a court,

    for the purposes of proceedings in a particular cause or matter.

(2) Information held by a public authority is exempt information if it is held only by virtue of being contained in—

(a) any document placed in the custody of a person conducting an inquiry or arbitration, for the purposes of the inquiry or arbitration, or

(b) any document created by a person conducting an inquiry or arbitration, for the purposes of the inquiry or arbitration.

(3) The duty to confirm or deny does not arise in relation to information which is (or if it were held by the public authority would be) exempt information by virtue of this section.

(4) In this section—

(a) "court" includes any tribunal or body exercising the judicial power of the State,

(b) "proceedings in a particular cause or matter" includes any inquest or post-mortem examination,

(c) "inquiry" means any inquiry or hearing held under any provision contained in, or made under, an enactment, and

(d) except in relation to Scotland, "arbitration" means any arbitration to which Part I of the Arbitration Act 1996 applies.

Definitions For "public authority", see s 3(1); as to "body" and "enactment" and for "information", see s 84.
References See paras 2.5, 4.53–4.55, 6.3.

33 Audit functions

(1) This section applies to any public authority which has functions in relation to—

(a) the audit of the accounts of other public authorities, or

(b) the examination of the economy, efficiency and effectiveness with which other public authorities use their resources in discharging their functions.

(2) Information held by a public authority to which this section applies is exempt information if its disclosure would, or would be likely to, prejudice the exercise of any of the authority's functions in relation to any of the matters referred to in subsection (1).

(3) The duty to confirm or deny does not arise in relation to a public authority to which this section applies if, or to the extent that, compliance with section 1(1)(a) would, or would be likely to, prejudice the exercise of any of the authority's functions in relation to any of the matters referred to in subsection (1).

Definitions For "the duty to confirm or deny", see s 1(6); for "public authority", see s 3(1); for "information", see s 84.
References See paras 2.5, 4.56, 4.57, 6.3.

34 Parliamentary privilege

(1) Information is exempt information if exemption from section 1(1)(b) is required for the purpose of avoiding an infringement of the privileges of either House of Parliament.

(2) The duty to confirm or deny does not apply if, or to the extent that, exemption from section 1(1)(a) is required for the purpose of avoiding an infringement of the privileges of either House of Parliament.

(3)   A certificate signed by the appropriate authority certifying that exemption from section 1(1)(b), or from section 1(1)(a) and (b), is, or at any time was, required for the purpose of avoiding an infringement of the privileges of either House of Parliament shall be conclusive evidence of that fact.

(4)   In subsection (3) "the appropriate authority" means—
  (a)   in relation to the House of Commons, the Speaker of that House, and
  (b)   in relation to the House of Lords, the Clerk of the Parliaments.

Definitions   For "the duty to confirm or deny", see s 1(6); for "information", see s 84.
References   See paras 2.5, 4.58.

---

35 Formulation of government policy, etc

(1)   Information held by a government department or by the National Assembly for Wales is exempt information if it relates to—
  (a)   the formulation or development of government policy,
  (b)   Ministerial communications,
  (c)   the provision of advice by any of the Law Officers or any request for the provision of such advice, or
  (d)   the operation of any Ministerial private office.

(2)   Once a decision as to government policy has been taken, any statistical information used to provide an informed background to the taking of the decision is not to be regarded—
  (a)   for the purposes of subsection (1)(a), as relating to the formulation or development of government policy, or
  (b)   for the purposes of subsection (1)(b), as relating to Ministerial communications.

(3)   The duty to confirm or deny does not arise in relation to information which is (or if it were held by the public authority would be) exempt information by virtue of subsection (1).

(4)   In making any determination required by section 2(1)(b) or (2)(b) in relation to information which is exempt information by virtue of subsection (1)(a), regard shall be had to the particular public interest in the disclosure of factual information which has been used, or is intended to be used, to provide an informed background to decision-taking.

(5)   In this section—
  "government policy" includes the policy of the Executive Committee of the Northern Ireland Assembly and the policy of the National Assembly for Wales;
  "the Law Officers" means the Attorney General, the Solicitor General, the Advocate General for Scotland, the Lord Advocate, the Solicitor General for Scotland and the Attorney General for Northern Ireland;
  "Ministerial communications" means any communications—
    (a)   between Ministers of the Crown,
    (b)   between Northern Ireland Ministers, including Northern Ireland junior Ministers, or

(c)   between Assembly Secretaries, including the Assembly First Secretary,

and includes, in particular, proceedings of the Cabinet or of any committee of the Cabinet, proceedings of the Executive Committee of the Northern Ireland Assembly, and proceedings of the executive committee of the National Assembly for Wales;

"Ministerial private office" means any part of a government department which provides personal administrative support to a Minister of the Crown, to a Northern Ireland Minister or a Northern Ireland junior Minister or any part of the administration of the National Assembly for Wales providing personal administrative support to the Assembly First Secretary or an Assembly Secretary;

"Northern Ireland junior Minister" means a member of the Northern Ireland Assembly appointed as a junior Minister under section 19 of the Northern Ireland Act 1998.

Definitions   For "the duty to confirm or deny", see s 1(6); for "public authority", see s 3(1); as to "government department" and for "information", "Ministers of the Crown" and "Northern Ireland Ministers", see s 84.
References   See paras 2.5, 4.11, 4.59–4.64, 4.66, 6.3.

---

36 Prejudice to effective conduct of public affairs

(1)   This section applies to—
    (a)   information which is held by a government department or by the National Assembly for Wales and is not exempt information by virtue of section 35, and
    (b)   information which is held by any other public authority.

(2)   Information to which this section applies is exempt information if, in the reasonable opinion of a qualified person, disclosure of the information under this Act—
    (a)   would, or would be likely to, prejudice—
        (i)   the maintenance of the convention of the collective responsibility of Ministers of the Crown, or
        (ii)   the work of the Executive Committee of the Northern Ireland Assembly, or
        (iii)   the work of the executive committee of the National Assembly for Wales,
    (b)   would, or would be likely to, inhibit—
        (i)   the free and frank provision of advice, or
        (ii)   the free and frank exchange of views for the purposes of deliberation, or
    (c)   would otherwise prejudice, or would be likely otherwise to prejudice, the effective conduct of public affairs.

(3)   The duty to confirm or deny does not arise in relation to information to which this section applies (or would apply if held by the public authority) if, or to the extent that, in the reasonable opinion of a qualified person, compliance with section 1(1)(a) would, or would be likely to, have any of the effects mentioned in subsection (2).

(4)   In relation to statistical information, subsections (2) and (3) shall have effect with the omission of the words "in the reasonable opinion of a qualified person".

(5)   In subsections (2) and (3) "qualified person"—

    (a)   in relation to information held by a government department in the charge of a Minister of the Crown, means any Minister of the Crown,

    (b)   in relation to information held by a Northern Ireland department, means the Northern Ireland Minister in charge of the department,

    (c)   in relation to information held by any other government department, means the commissioners or other person in charge of that department,

    (d)   in relation to information held by the House of Commons, means the Speaker of that House,

    (e)   in relation to information held by the House of Lords, means the Clerk of the Parliaments,

    (f)   in relation to information held by the Northern Ireland Assembly, means the Presiding Officer,

    (g)   in relation to information held by the National Assembly for Wales, means the Assembly First Secretary,

    (h)   in relation to information held by any Welsh public authority other than the Auditor General for Wales, means—

        (i)   the public authority, or

        (ii)   any officer or employee of the authority authorised by the Assembly First Secretary,

    (i)   in relation to information held by the National Audit Office, means the Comptroller and Auditor General,

    (j)   in relation to information held by the Northern Ireland Audit Office, means the Comptroller and Auditor General for Northern Ireland,

    (k)   in relation to information held by the Auditor General for Wales, means the Auditor General for Wales,

    (l)   in relation to information held by any Northern Ireland public authority other than the Northern Ireland Audit Office, means—

        (i)   the public authority, or

        (ii)   any officer or employee of the authority authorised by the First Minister and deputy First Minister in Northern Ireland acting jointly,

    (m)   in relation to information held by the Greater London Authority, means the Mayor of London,

    (n)   in relation to information held by a functional body within the meaning of the Greater London Authority Act 1999, means the chairman of that functional body, and

    (o)   in relation to information held by any public authority not falling within any of paragraphs (a) to (n), means—

        (i)   a Minister of the Crown,

        (ii)   the public authority, if authorised for the purposes of this section by a Minister of the Crown, or

        (iii)   any officer or employee of the public authority who is authorised for the purposes of this section by a Minister of the Crown.

(6)   Any authorisation for the purposes of this section—
    (a)   may relate to a specified person or to persons falling within a specified class,
    (b)   may be general or limited to particular classes of case, and
    (c)   may be granted subject to conditions.

(7)   A certificate signed by the qualified person referred to in subsection (5)(d) or (e) above certifying that in his reasonable opinion—
    (a)   disclosure of information held by either House of Parliament, or
    (b)   compliance with section 1(1)(a) by either House,
would, or would be likely to, have any of the effects mentioned in subsection (2) shall be conclusive evidence of that fact.

Definitions   For "the duty to confirm or deny", see s 1(6); for "public authority", see s 3(1); for "Welsh public authority", see s 83; as to "government department" and for "information", "Ministers of the Crown", "Northern Ireland Minister" and "Northern Ireland public authority", see s 84.
References   See paras 2.5, 4.65–4.71, 6.3.

37 Communications with Her Majesty, etc and honours

(1)   Information is exempt information if it relates to—
    (a)   communications with Her Majesty, with other members of the Royal Family or with the Royal Household, or
    (b)   the conferring by the Crown of any honour or dignity.

(2)   The duty to confirm or deny does not arise in relation to information which is (or if it were held by the public authority would be) exempt information by virtue of subsection (1).

Definitions   For "the duty to confirm or deny", see s 1(6); for "information", see s 84.
References   See paras 2.5, 4.73, 6.3, 6.4.

38 Health and safety

(1)   Information is exempt information if its disclosure under this Act would, or would be likely to—
    (a)   endanger the physical or mental health of any individual, or
    (b)   endanger the safety of any individual.

(2)   The duty to confirm or deny does not arise if, or to the extent that, compliance with section 1(1)(a) would, or would be likely to, have either of the effects mentioned in subsection (1).

Definitions   For "the duty to confirm or deny", see s 1(6); for "information", see s 84.
References   See paras 2.5, 4.74.

39 Environmental information

(1)   Information is exempt information if the public authority holding it—
    (a)   is obliged by regulations under section 74 to make the information available to the public in accordance with the regulations, or

(b)   would be so obliged but for any exemption contained in the regulations.

(2)   The duty to confirm or deny does not arise in relation to information which is (or if it were held by the public authority would be) exempt information by virtue of subsection (1).

(3)   Subsection (1)(a) does not limit the generality of section 21(1).

Definitions   For "the duty to confirm or deny", see s 1(6); for "public authority", see s 2(1); for "information", see s 84.
References   See paras 2.5, 4.75, 4.76.

40 Personal information

(1)   Any information to which a request for information relates is exempt information if it constitutes personal data of which the applicant is the data subject.

(2)   Any information to which a request for information relates is also exempt information if—

   (a)   it constitutes personal data which do not fall within subsection (1), and

   (b)   either the first or the second condition below is satisfied.

(3)   The first condition is—

   (a)   in a case where the information falls within any of paragraphs (a) to (d) of the definition of "data" in section 1(1) of the Data Protection Act 1998, that the disclosure of the information to a member of the public otherwise than under this Act would contravene—

      (i)   any of the data protection principles, or

      (ii)   section 10 of that Act (right to prevent processing likely to cause damage or distress), and

   (b)   in any other case, that the disclosure of the information to a member of the public otherwise than under this Act would contravene any of the data protection principles if the exemptions in section 33A(1) of the Data Protection Act 1998 (which relate to manual data held by public authorities) were disregarded.

(4)   The second condition is that by virtue of any provision of Part IV of the Data Protection Act 1998 the information is exempt from section 7(1)(c) of that Act (data subject's right of access to personal data).

(5)   The duty to confirm or deny—

   (a)   does not arise in relation to information which is (or if it were held by the public authority would be) exempt information by virtue of subsection (1), and

   (b)   does not arise in relation to other information if or to the extent that either—

      (i)   the giving to a member of the public of the confirmation or denial that would have to be given to comply with section 1(1)(a) would (apart from this Act) contravene any of the data protection principles or section 10 of the Data Protection Act 1998 or would do so if the exemptions in section 33A(1) of that Act were disregarded, or

(ii) by virtue of any provision of Part IV of the Data Protection Act 1998 the information is exempt from section 7(1)(a) of that Act (data subject's right to be informed whether personal data being processed).

(6) In determining for the purposes of this section whether anything done before 24th October 2007 would contravene any of the data protection principles, the exemptions in Part III of Schedule 8 to the Data Protection Act 1998 shall be disregarded.

(7) In this section—

"the data protection principles" means the principles set out in Part I of Schedule 1 to the Data Protection Act 1998, as read subject to Part II of that Schedule and section 27(1) of that Act;

"data subject" has the same meaning as in section 1(1) of that Act;

"personal data" has the same meaning as in section 1(1) of that Act.

Definitions   For "the duty to confirm or deny", see s 1(6); for "public authority", see s 3(1); for "request for information", see s 8; for "applicant" and "information", see s 84.
References   See paras 2.5, 4.77–4.82, 7.11.

41 Information provided in confidence

(1) Information is exempt information if—
  (a) it was obtained by the public authority from any other person (including another public authority), and
  (b) the disclosure of the information to the public (otherwise than under this Act) by the public authority holding it would constitute a breach of confidence actionable by that or any other person.

(2) The duty to confirm or deny does not arise if, or to the extent that, the confirmation or denial that would have to be given to comply with section 1(1)(a) would (apart from this Act) constitute an actionable breach of confidence.

Definitions   For "the duty to confirm or deny", see s 1(6); for "public authority", see s 3(1); for "information", see s 84.
References   See paras 2.5, 4.84.

42 Legal professional privilege

(1) Information in respect of which a claim to legal professional privilege or, in Scotland, to confidentiality of communications could be maintained in legal proceedings is exempt information.

(2) The duty to confirm or deny does not arise if, or to the extent that, compliance with section 1(1)(a) would involve the disclosure of any information (whether or not already recorded) in respect of which such a claim could be maintained in legal proceedings.

Definitions   For "the duty to confirm or deny", see s 1(6); for "information", see s 84.
References   See paras 2.5, 4.86, 6.3.

43 Commercial interests

(1)   Information is exempt information if it constitutes a trade secret.

(2)   Information is exempt information if its disclosure under this Act would, or would be likely to, prejudice the commercial interests of any person (including the public authority holding it).

(3)   The duty to confirm or deny does not arise if, or to the extent that, compliance with section 1(1)(a) would, or would be likely to, prejudice the interests mentioned in subsection (2).

Definitions   For "the duty to confirm or deny", see s 1(6); for "public authority", see s 3(1); for "information", see s 84.
References   See paras 2.5, 4.87, 4.89, 6.3.

44 Prohibitions on disclosure

(1)   Information is exempt information if its disclosure (otherwise than under this Act) by the public authority holding it—
    (a)   is prohibited by or under any enactment,
    (b)   is incompatible with any Community obligation, or
    (c)   would constitute or be punishable as a contempt of court.

(2)   The duty to confirm or deny does not arise if the confirmation or denial that would have to be given to comply with section 1(1)(a) would (apart from this Act) fall within any of paragraphs (a) to (c) of subsection (1).

Definitions   For "the duty to confirm or deny", see s 1(6); for "public authority", see s 3(1); as to "enactment", and for "information", see s 84.
References   See paras 2.5, 4.90, 6.9.

PART III
GENERAL FUNCTIONS OF . . . LORD CHANCELLOR AND INFORMATION COMMISSIONER

45 Issue of code of practice by [Lord Chancellor]

(1)   The [Lord Chancellor] shall issue, and may from time to time revise, a code of practice providing guidance to public authorities as to the practice which it would, in his opinion, be desirable for them to follow in connection with the discharge of the authorities' functions under Part I.

(2)   The code of practice must, in particular, include provision relating to—
    (a)   the provision of advice and assistance by public authorities to persons who propose to make, or have made, requests for information to them,
    (b)   the transfer of requests by one public authority to another public authority by which the information requested is or may be held,
    (c)   consultation with persons to whom the information requested relates or persons whose interests are likely to be affected by the disclosure of information,
    (d)   the inclusion in contracts entered into by public authorities of terms relating to the disclosure of information, and

> (e)   the provision by public authorities of procedures for dealing with complaints about the handling by them of requests for information.

(3)   The code may make different provision for different public authorities.

(4)   Before issuing or revising any code under this section, the [Lord Chancellor] shall consult the Commissioner.

(5)   The [Lord Chancellor] shall lay before each House of Parliament any code or revised code made under this section.

Definitions   For "public authorities", see s 3(1); for "requests for information", see s 8; for "the Commissioner" and "information", see s 84.
Amendments   Part Heading: words omitted repealed by the Transfer of Functions (Miscellaneous) Order 2001, SI 2001/3500, art 8, Sch 2, para 8(1)(h).
Section heading and sub-ss (1), (4), (5): words in square brackets substituted by SI 2001/3500, art 8, Sch 2, para 8(1)(h).
References   See paras 2.10, 2.18, 3.19, 5.2, 5.8–5.10, 5.16, 5.18.

---

46 Issue of code of practice by Lord Chancellor

(1)   The Lord Chancellor shall issue, and may from time to time revise, a code of practice providing guidance to relevant authorities as to the practice which it would, in his opinion, be desirable for them to follow in connection with the keeping, management and destruction of their records.

(2)   For the purpose of facilitating the performance by the Public Record Office, the Public Record Office of Northern Ireland and other public authorities of their functions under this Act in relation to records which are public records for the purposes of the Public Records Act 1958 or the Public Records Act (Northern Ireland) 1923, the code may also include guidance as to—

> (a)   the practice to be adopted in relation to the transfer of records under section 3(4) of the Public Records Act 1958 or section 3 of the Public Records Act (Northern Ireland) 1923, and
> (b)   the practice of reviewing records before they are transferred under those provisions.

(3)   In exercising his functions under this section, the Lord Chancellor shall have regard to the public interest in allowing public access to information held by relevant authorities.

(4)   The code may make different provision for different relevant authorities.

(5)   Before issuing or revising any code under this section the Lord Chancellor shall consult—

> (a)   . . .
> (b)   the Commissioner, and
> (c)   in relation to Northern Ireland, the appropriate Northern Ireland Minister.

(6)   The Lord Chancellor shall lay before each House of Parliament any code or revised code made under this section.

(7)   In this section "relevant authority" means—

> (a)   any public authority, and

      (b)   any office or body which is not a public authority but whose administrative and departmental records are public records for the purposes of the Public Records Act 1958 or the Public Records Act (Northern Ireland) 1923.

Definitions   For "public authorities", see s 3(1); as to "body" and for "appropriate Northern Ireland Minister", "the Commissioner" and "the Northern Ireland Minister", see s 84.
Amendments   Sub-s 5: para (a) repealed by the Transfer of Functions (Miscellaneous) Order 2001, SI 2001/3500, art 8, Sch 2, para 8(2).
References   See paras 2.10, 3.8, 5.6, 5.8–5.10, 5.18.

47 General functions of Commissioner

(1)   It shall be the duty of the Commissioner to promote the following of good practice by public authorities and, in particular, so to perform his functions under this Act as to promote the observance by public authorities of—
      (a)   the requirements of this Act, and
      (b)   the provisions of the codes of practice under sections 45 and 46.

(2)   The Commissioner shall arrange for the dissemination in such form and manner as he considers appropriate of such information as it may appear to him expedient to give to the public—
      (a)   about the operation of this Act,
      (b)   about good practice, and
      (c)   about other matters within the scope of his functions under this Act,
and may give advice to any person as to any of those matters.

(3)   The Commissioner may, with the consent of any public authority, assess whether that authority is following good practice.

(4)   The Commissioner may charge such sums as he may with the consent of the [Lord Chancellor] determine for any services provided by the Commissioner under this section.

(5)   The Commissioner shall from time to time as he considers appropriate—
      (a)   consult the Keeper of Public Records about the promotion by the Commissioner of the observance by public authorities of the provisions of the code of practice under section 46 in relation to records which are public records for the purposes of the Public Records Act 1958, and
      (b)   consult the Deputy Keeper of the Records of Northern Ireland about the promotion by the Commissioner of the observance by public authorities of those provisions in relation to records which are public records for the purposes of the Public Records Act (Northern Ireland) 1923.

(6)   In this section "good practice", in relation to a public authority, means such practice in the discharge of its functions under this Act as appears to the Commissioner to be desirable, and includes (but is not limited to) compliance with the requirements of this Act and the provisions of the codes of practice under sections 45 and 46.

Definitions   For "public authorities", see s 3(1); for "the Commissioner" and "information", see s 84.
Amendments: Sub-s (4): words in square brackets substituted by the Transfer of Functions (Miscellaneous) Order 2001, SI 2001/3500, art 8, Sch 2, para 8(1)(i).
References   See paras 2.10, 5.8, 5.9.

48 Recommendations as to good practice

(1)   If it appears to the Commissioner that the practice of a public authority in relation to the exercise of its functions under this Act does not conform with that proposed in the codes of practice under sections 45 and 46, he may give to the authority a recommendation (in this section referred to as a "practice recommendation") specifying the steps which ought in his opinion to be taken for promoting such conformity.

(2)   A practice recommendation must be given in writing and must refer to the particular provisions of the code of practice with which, in the Commissioner's opinion, the public authority's practice does not conform.

(3)   Before giving to a public authority other than the Public Record Office a practice recommendation which relates to conformity with the code of practice under section 46 in respect of records which are public records for the purposes of the Public Records Act 1958, the Commissioner shall consult the Keeper of Public Records.

(4)   Before giving to a public authority other than the Public Record Office of Northern Ireland a practice recommendation which relates to conformity with the code of practice under section 46 in respect of records which are public records for the purposes of the Public Records Act (Northern Ireland) 1923, the Commissioner shall consult the Deputy Keeper of the Records of Northern Ireland.

Definitions   For "public authorities", see s 3(1); for "the Commissioner", see s 84.
References   See paras 2.10, 5.10, 6.11.

49 Reports to be laid before Parliament

(1)   The Commissioner shall lay annually before each House of Parliament a general report on the exercise of his functions under this Act.

(2)   The Commissioner may from time to time lay before each House of Parliament such other reports with respect to those functions as he thinks fit.

Definitions   For "the Commissioner", see s 84.
References   See para 5.11.

PART IV
ENFORCEMENT

50 Application for decision by Commissioner

(1)   Any person (in this section referred to as "the complainant") may apply to the Commissioner for a decision whether, in any specified respect, a request for information made by the complainant to a public authority has been dealt with in accordance with the requirements of Part I.

(2)   On receiving an application under this section, the Commissioner shall make a decision unless it appears to him—
    (a)   that the complainant has not exhausted any complaints procedure which is provided by the public authority in conformity with the code of practice under section 45,
    (b)   that there has been undue delay in making the application,
    (c)   that the application is frivolous or vexatious, or
    (d)   that the application has been withdrawn or abandoned.

(3)   Where the Commissioner has received an application under this section, he shall either—

    (a)   notify the complainant that he has not made any decision under this section as a result of the application and of his grounds for not doing so, or

    (b)   serve notice of his decision (in this Act referred to as a "decision notice") on the complainant and the public authority.

(4)   Where the Commissioner decides that a public authority—

    (a)   has failed to communicate information, or to provide confirmation or denial, in a case where it is required to do so by section 1(1), or

    (b)   has failed to comply with any of the requirements of sections 11 and 17,

the decision notice must specify the steps which must be taken by the authority for complying with that requirement and the period within which they must be taken.

(5)   A decision notice must contain particulars of the right of appeal conferred by section 57.

(6)   Where a decision notice requires steps to be taken by the public authority within a specified period, the time specified in the notice must not expire before the end of the period within which an appeal can be brought against the notice and, if such an appeal is brought, no step which is affected by the appeal need be taken pending the determination or withdrawal of the appeal.

(7)   This section has effect subject to section 53.

Definitions   For "public authority", see s 3(1); for "request for information", see s 8; for "applicant", "the Commissioner" and "information", see s 84.
References   See paras 2.11, 2.22, 2.27, 5.4, 5.14–5.16, 5.18, 5.24, 5.28, 5.37.

51 Information notices

(1)   If the Commissioner—

    (a)   has received an application under section 50, or

    (b)   reasonably requires any information—

        (i)   for the purpose of determining whether a public authority has complied or is complying with any of the requirements of Part I, or

        (ii)   for the purpose of determining whether the practice of a public authority in relation to the exercise of its functions under this Act conforms with that proposed in the codes of practice under sections 45 and 46,

he may serve the authority with a notice (in this Act referred to as "an information notice") requiring it, within such time as is specified in the notice, to furnish the Commissioner, in such form as may be so specified, with such information relating to the application, to compliance with Part I or to conformity with the code of practice as is so specified.

(2)   An information notice must contain—

    (a)   in a case falling within subsection (1)(a), a statement that the Commissioner has received an application under section 50, or

(b) in a case falling within subsection (1)(b), a statement—

    (i) that the Commissioner regards the specified information as relevant for either of the purposes referred to in subsection (1)(b), and

    (ii) of his reasons for regarding that information as relevant for that purpose.

(3) An information notice must also contain particulars of the right of appeal conferred by section 57.

(4) The time specified in an information notice must not expire before the end of the period within which an appeal can be brought against the notice and, if such an appeal is brought, the information need not be furnished pending the determination or withdrawal of the appeal.

(5) An authority shall not be required by virtue of this section to furnish the Commissioner with any information in respect of—

(a) any communication between a professional legal adviser and his client in connection with the giving of legal advice to the client with respect to his obligations, liabilities or rights under this Act, or

(b) any communication between a professional legal adviser and his client, or between such an adviser or his client and any other person, made in connection with or in contemplation of proceedings under or arising out of this Act (including proceedings before the Tribunal) and for the purposes of such proceedings.

(6) In subsection (5) references to the client of a professional legal adviser include references to any person representing such a client.

(7) The Commissioner may cancel an information notice by written notice to the authority on which it was served.

(8) In this section "information" includes unrecorded information.

Definitions   For "public authority", see s 3(1); for "the Commissioner", "information" and "the Tribunal", see s 84.
References   See paras 3.6, 5.17–5.19, 5.24.

52 Enforcement notices

(1) If the Commissioner is satisfied that a public authority has failed to comply with any of the requirements of Part I, the Commissioner may serve the authority with a notice (in this Act referred to as "an enforcement notice") requiring the authority to take, within such time as may be specified in the notice, such steps as may be so specified for complying with those requirements.

(2) An enforcement notice must contain—

(a) a statement of the requirement or requirements of Part I with which the Commissioner is satisfied that the public authority has failed to comply and his reasons for reaching that conclusion, and

(b) particulars of the right of appeal conferred by section 57.

(3)   An enforcement notice must not require any of the provisions of the notice to be complied with before the end of the period within which an appeal can be brought against the notice and, if such an appeal is brought, the notice need not be complied with pending the determination or withdrawal of the appeal.

(4)   The Commissioner may cancel an enforcement notice by written notice to the authority on which it was served.

(5)   This section has effect subject to section 53.

Definitions   For "public authority", see s 3(1); for "applicant", "the Commissioner" and "information", see s 84.
References   See paras 2.11, 2.27, 5.20, 5.24.

53 Exception from duty to comply with decision notice or enforcement notice

(1)   This section applies to a decision notice or enforcement notice which—
  (a)   is served on—
      (i)   a government department,
      (ii)   the National Assembly for Wales, or
      (iii)   any public authority designated for the purposes of this section by an order made by the [Lord Chancellor], and
  (b)   relates to a failure, in respect of one or more requests for information—
      (i)   to comply with section 1(1)(a) in respect of information which falls within any provision of Part II stating that the duty to confirm or deny does not arise, or
      (ii)   to comply with section 1(1)(b) in respect of exempt information.

(2)   A decision notice or enforcement notice to which this section applies shall cease to have effect if, not later than the twentieth working day following the effective date, the accountable person in relation to that authority gives the Commissioner a certificate signed by him stating that he has on reasonable grounds formed the opinion that, in respect of the request or requests concerned, there was no failure falling within subsection (1)(b).

(3)   Where the accountable person gives a certificate to the Commissioner under subsection (2) he shall as soon as practicable thereafter lay a copy of the certificate before—
  (a)   each House of Parliament,
  (b)   the Northern Ireland Assembly, in any case where the certificate relates to a decision notice or enforcement notice which has been served on a Northern Ireland department or any Northern Ireland public authority, or
  (c)   the National Assembly for Wales, in any case where the certificate relates to a decision notice or enforcement notice which has been served on the National Assembly for Wales or any Welsh public authority.

(4)   In subsection (2) "the effective date", in relation to a decision notice or enforcement notice, means—
  (a)   the day on which the notice was given to the public authority, or

(b)   where an appeal under section 57 is brought, the day on which that appeal (or any further appeal arising out of it) is determined or withdrawn.

(5)   Before making an order under subsection (1)(a)(iii), the [Lord Chancellor] shall—
    (a)   if the order relates to a Welsh public authority, consult the National Assembly for Wales,
    (b)   if the order relates to the Northern Ireland Assembly, consult the Presiding Officer of that Assembly, and
    (c)   if the order relates to a Northern Ireland public authority, consult the First Minister and deputy First Minister in Northern Ireland.

(6)   Where the accountable person gives a certificate to the Commissioner under subsection (2) in relation to a decision notice, the accountable person shall, on doing so or as soon as reasonably practicable after doing so, inform the person who is the complainant for the purposes of section 50 of the reasons for his opinion.

(7)   The accountable person is not obliged to provide information under subsection (6) if, or to the extent that, compliance with that subsection would involve the disclosure of exempt information.

(8)   In this section "the accountable person"—
    (a)   in relation to a Northern Ireland department or any Northern Ireland public authority, means the First Minister and deputy First Minister in Northern Ireland acting jointly,
    (b)   in relation to the National Assembly for Wales or any Welsh public authority, means the Assembly First Secretary, and
    (c)   in relation to any other public authority, means—
        (i)   a Minister of the Crown who is a member of the Cabinet, or
       (ii)   the Attorney General, the Advocate General for Scotland or the Attorney General for Northern Ireland.

(9)   In this section "working day" has the same meaning as in section 10.

Definitions   For "the duty to confirm or deny", see s 1(6); for "public authority", see s 3(1); for "decision notice", see s 50; for "enforcement notice", see s 52; for "the Commissioner", "exempt information", "government department", "information", "Minister of the Crown" and "Northern Ireland public authority", see s 80; for "Welsh public authority", see s 83.
Amendments: Sub-ss (1), (5): words in square brackets substituted by the Transfer of Functions (Miscellaneous) Order 2001, SI 2001/3500, art 8, Sch 2, para 8(1)(j).
References   See paras 2.11, 5.13, 5.23, 5.25–5.30, 5.37.

---

54 Failure to comply with notice

(1)   If a public authority has failed to comply with—
    (a)   so much of a decision notice as requires steps to be taken,
    (b)   an information notice, or
    (c)   an enforcement notice,
the Commissioner may certify in writing to the court that the public authority has failed to comply with that notice.

(2)   For the purposes of this section, a public authority which, in purported compliance with an information notice—
    (a)   makes a statement which it knows to be false in a material respect, or
    (b)   recklessly makes a statement which is false in a material respect,
is to be taken to have failed to comply with the notice.

(3)   Where a failure to comply is certified under subsection (1), the court may inquire into the matter and, after hearing any witness who may be produced against or on behalf of the public authority, and after hearing any statement that may be offered in defence, deal with the authority as if it had committed a contempt of court.

(4)   In this section "the court" means the High Court or, in Scotland, the Court of Session.

Definitions   For "public authority", see s 3(1); for "decision notice", see s 50; for "information notice", see s 51; for "enforcement notice", see s 52; for "the Commissioner", see s 84.
References   See paras 2.27, 5.13, 5.22, 5.31, 5.34, 5.37.

55 Powers of entry and inspection

Schedule 3 (powers of entry and inspection) has effect.

References   See para 5.32.

56 No action against public authority

(1)   This Act does not confer any right of action in civil proceedings in respect of any failure to comply with any duty imposed by or under this Act.

(2)   Subsection (1) does not affect the powers of the Commissioner under section 54.

Definitions   For "the Commissioner", see s 84.
References   See para 5.34.

PART V
APPEALS

57 Appeal against notices served under Part IV

(1)   Where a decision notice has been served, the complainant or the public authority may appeal to the Tribunal against the notice.

(2)   A public authority on which an information notice or an enforcement notice has been served by the Commissioner may appeal to the Tribunal against the notice.

(3)   In relation to a decision notice or enforcement notice which relates—
    (a)   to information to which section 66 applies, and
    (b)   to a matter which by virtue of subsection (3) or (4) of that section falls to be determined by the responsible authority instead of the appropriate records authority,
subsections (1) and (2) shall have effect as if the reference to the public authority were a reference to the public authority or the responsible authority.

Definitions   For "public authority", see s 3(1); for "the complainant" and "decision notice", see s 50; for "information notice", see s 51; for "enforcement notice", see s 52; for "the Commissioner", "information", "responsible authority" and "the Tribunal", see s 84.
References   See paras 2.12, 2.22, 2.28, 5.24, 5.28, 5.36, 5.37.

58 Determination of appeals

(1)   If on an appeal under section 57 the Tribunal considers—

   (a)   that the notice against which the appeal is brought is not in accordance with the law, or

   (b)   to the extent that the notice involved an exercise of discretion by the Commissioner, that he ought to have exercised his discretion differently,

the Tribunal shall allow the appeal or substitute such other notice as could have been served by the Commissioner; and in any other case the Tribunal shall dismiss the appeal.

(2)   On such an appeal, the Tribunal may review any finding of fact on which the notice in question was based.

Definitions   For "the Commissioner" and "the Tribunal", see s 84.
References   See paras 5.38, 5.39.

59 Appeals from decision of Tribunal

Any party to an appeal to the Tribunal under section 57 may appeal from the decision of the Tribunal on a point of law to the appropriate court; and that court shall be—

   (a)   the High Court of Justice in England if the address of the public authority is in England or Wales,

   (b)   the Court of Session if that address is in Scotland, and

   (c)   the High Court of Justice in Northern Ireland if that address is in Northern Ireland.

Definitions   For "public authority", see s 3(1); for "the Tribunal", see s 84.
References   See paras 2.12, 2.22, 5.40.

60 Appeals against national security certificate

(1)   Where a certificate under section 23(2) or 24(3) has been issued—

   (a)   the Commissioner, or

   (b)   any applicant whose request for information is affected by the issue of the certificate,

may appeal to the Tribunal against the certificate.

(2)   If on an appeal under subsection (1) relating to a certificate under section 23(2), the Tribunal finds that the information referred to in the certificate was not exempt information by virtue of section 23(1), the Tribunal may allow the appeal and quash the certificate.

(3)   If on an appeal under subsection (1) relating to a certificate under section 24(3), the Tribunal finds that, applying the principles applied by the court on an application for judicial review, the Minister did not have reasonable grounds for issuing the certificate, the Tribunal may allow the appeal and quash the certificate.

(4)   Where in any proceedings under this Act it is claimed by a public authority that a certificate under section 24(3) which identifies the information to which it applies by means of a general description applies to particular

information, any other party to the proceedings may appeal to the Tribunal on the ground that the certificate does not apply to the information in question and, subject to any determination under subsection (5), the certificate shall be conclusively presumed so to apply.

(5)   On any appeal under subsection (4), the Tribunal may determine that the certificate does not so apply.

Definitions   For "public authority", see s 3(1); for "request for information", see s 8; for "applicant", "the Commissioner", "exempt information", "information" and "the Tribunal", see s 84.
References   See paras 4.28–4.30, 4.32, 4.35, 4.38, 4.58, 5.41–5.46.

61 Appeal proceedings

(1)   Schedule 4 (which contains amendments of Schedule 6 to the Data Protection Act 1998 relating to appeal proceedings) has effect.

(2)   Accordingly, the provisions of Schedule 6 to the Data Protection Act 1998 have effect (so far as applicable) in relation to appeals under this Part.

References   See para 5.47.

PART VI
HISTORICAL RECORDS AND RECORDS IN PUBLIC RECORD OFFICE OR PUBLIC RECORD OFFICE OF NORTHERN IRELAND

62 Interpretation of Part VI

(1)   For the purposes of this Part, a record becomes a "historical record" at the end of the period of thirty years beginning with the year following that in which it was created.

(2)   Where records created at different dates are for administrative purposes kept together in one file or other assembly, all the records in that file or other assembly are to be treated for the purposes of this Part as having been created when the latest of those records was created.

(3)   In this Part "year" means a calendar year.

References   See para 6.2.

63 Removal of exemptions: historical records generally

(1)   Information contained in a historical record cannot be exempt information by virtue of section 28, 30(1), 32, 33, 35, 36, 37(1)(a), 42 or 43.

(2)   Compliance with section 1(1)(a) in relation to a historical record is not to be taken to be capable of having any of the effects referred to in section 28(3), 33(3), 36(3), 42(2) or 43(3).

(3)   Information cannot be exempt information by virtue of section 37(1)(b) after the end of the period of sixty years beginning with the year following that in which the record containing the information was created.

(4)   Information cannot be exempt information by virtue of section 31 after the end of the period of one hundred years beginning with the year following that in which the record containing the information was created.

(5)   Compliance with section 1(1)(a) in relation to any record is not to be taken, at any time after the end of the period of one hundred years beginning with the year following that in which the record was created, to be capable of prejudicing any of the matters referred to in section 31(1).

Definitions   For "historical record" and "year", see s 61; for "exempt information" and "information", see s 84.
References   See paras 6.3, 6.4.

64 Removal of exemptions: historical records in public record offices

(1)   Information contained in a historical record in the Public Record Office or the Public Record Office of Northern Ireland cannot be exempt information by virtue of section 21 or 22.

(2)   In relation to any information falling within section 23(1) which is contained in a historical record in the Public Record Office or the Public Record Office of Northern Ireland, section 2(3) shall have effect with the omission of the reference to section 23.

Definitions   For "historical record", see s 62; for "information", see s 84.
References   See para 6.5.

65 Decisions as to refusal of discretionary disclosure of historical records

(1)   Before refusing a request for information relating to information which is contained in a historical record and is exempt information only by virtue of a provision not specified in section 2(3), a public authority shall—
>   (a)   if the historical record is a public record within the meaning of the Public Records Act 1958, consult the Lord Chancellor, or
>   (b)   if the historical record is a public record to which the Public Records Act (Northern Ireland) 1923 applies, consult the appropriate Northern Ireland Minister.

(2)   This section does not apply to information to which section 66 applies.

Definitions   For "public authority", see s 3(1); for "request for information", see s 8; for "historical record", see s 62; for "exempt information", "information" and "Northern Ireland Minister", see s 84.
References   See para 6.6.

66 Decisions relating to certain transferred public records

(1)   This section applies to any information which is (or, if it existed, would be) contained in a transferred public record, other than information which the responsible authority has designated as open information for the purposes of this section.

(2)   Before determining whether—
>   (a)   information to which this section applies falls within any provision of Part II relating to the duty to confirm or deny, or

(b)　information to which this section applies is exempt information,

the appropriate records authority shall consult the responsible authority.

(3)　Where information to which this section applies falls within a provision of Part II relating to the duty to confirm or deny but does not fall within any of the provisions of that Part relating to that duty which are specified in subsection (3) of section 2, any question as to the application of subsection (1)(b) of that section is to be determined by the responsible authority instead of the appropriate records authority.

(4)　Where any information to which this section applies is exempt information only by virtue of any provision of Part II not specified in subsection (3) of section 2, any question as to the application of subsection (2)(b) of that section is to be determined by the responsible authority instead of the appropriate records authority.

(5)　Before making by virtue of subsection (3) or (4) any determination that subsection (1)(b) or (2)(b) of section 2 applies, the responsible authority shall consult—

　　(a)　where the transferred public record is a public record within the meaning of the Public Records Act 1958, the Lord Chancellor, and

　　(b)　where the transferred public record is a public record to which the Public Records Act (Northern Ireland) 1923 applies, the appropriate Northern Ireland Minister.

(6)　Where the responsible authority in relation to information to which this section applies is not (apart from this subsection) a public authority, it shall be treated as being a public authority for the purposes of Parts III, IV and V of this Act so far as relating to—

　　(a)　the duty imposed by section 15(3), and

　　(b)　the imposition of any requirement to furnish information relating to compliance with Part I in connection with the information to which this section applies.

Definitions　For "the duty to confirm or deny", see s 1(6); for "public authority", see s 3(1); for "transferred public record", see s 15(4); for "responsible authority", see s 15(5); as to "government department", and for "appropriate records authority", "exempt information", "information", "Minister of the Crown" and "the Northern Ireland Minister", see s 84.
References　See paras 3.58, 6.6.

67　Amendments of public records legislation

Schedule 5 (which amends the Public Records Act 1958 and the Public Records Act (Northern Ireland) 1923) has effect.

PART VII
AMENDMENTS OF DATA PROTECTION ACT 1998

Amendments relating to personal information held by public authorities

68　Extension of meaning of "data"

(1)　Section 1 of the Data Protection Act 1998 (basic interpretative provisions) is amended in accordance with subsections (2) and (3).

(2)   In subsection (1)—

    (a)   in the definition of "data", the word "or" at the end of paragraph (c) is omitted and after paragraph (d) there is inserted "or

        (e)   is recorded information held by a public authority and does not fall within any of paragraphs (a) to (d);", and

    (b)   after the definition of "processing" there is inserted—

"public authority" has the same meaning as in the Freedom of Information Act 2000;".

(3)   After subsection (4) there is inserted—

"(5) In paragraph (e) of the definition of "data" in subsection (1), the reference to information "held" by a public authority shall be construed in accordance with section 3(2) of the Freedom of Information Act 2000.

(6)   Where section 7 of the Freedom of Information Act 2000 prevents Parts I to V of that Act from applying to certain information held by a public authority, that information is not to be treated for the purposes of paragraph (e) of the definition of "data" in subsection (1) as held by a public authority."

(4)   In section 56 of that Act (prohibition of requirement as to production of certain records), after subsection (6) there is inserted—

"(6A) A record is not a relevant record to the extent that it relates, or is to relate, only to personal data falling within paragraph (e) of the definition of "data" in section 1(1)."

(5)   In the Table in section 71 of that Act (index of defined expressions) after the entry relating to processing there is inserted—

"public authority   section 1(1)".

Definitions   For "public authority", see s 3(1); for "data" and "public authority", see the Data Protection Act 1998, s 1(1), as amended by s 68 above.
References   See para 7.10.

---

69 Right of access to unstructured personal data held by public authorities

(1)   In section 7(1) of the Data Protection Act 1998 (right of access to personal data), for "sections 8 and 9" there is substituted "sections 8, 9 and 9A".

(2)   After section 9 of that Act there is inserted—

"9A Unstructured personal data held by public authorities

(1)   In this section "unstructured personal data" means any personal data falling within paragraph (e) of the definition of "data" in section 1(1), other than information which is recorded as part of, or with the intention that it should form part of, any set of information relating to individuals to the extent that the set is structured by reference to individuals or by reference to criteria relating to individuals.

(2)   A public authority is not obliged to comply with subsection (1) of section 7 in relation to any unstructured personal data unless the request under that section contains a description of the data.

(3)   Even if the data are described by the data subject in his request, a public authority is not obliged to comply with subsection (1) of section 7 in relation to unstructured personal data if the authority estimates that the cost of complying with the request so far as relating to those data would exceed the appropriate limit.

(4)   Subsection (3) does not exempt the public authority from its obligation to comply with paragraph (a) of section 7(1) in relation to the unstructured personal data unless the estimated cost of complying with that paragraph alone in relation to those data would exceed the appropriate limit.

(5)   In subsections (3) and (4) "the appropriate limit" means such amount as may be prescribed by the Secretary of State by regulations, and different amounts may be prescribed in relation to different cases.

(6)   Any estimate for the purposes of this section must be made in accordance with regulations under section 12(5) of the Freedom of Information Act 2000."

(3)   In section 67(5) of that Act (statutory instruments subject to negative resolution procedure), in paragraph (c), for "or 9(3)" there is substituted ", 9(3) or 9A(5)".

Definitions   For "data", "data subject", "personal data" and "public authority", see the Data Protection Act 1998, s 1(1), as amended (definition "data" amended, definition "public authority" inserted) by s 68(1), (2); as to "recorded", see s 1(2)(a) of that Act.

---

70 Exemptions applicable to certain manual data held by public authorities

(1)   After section 33 of the Data Protection Act 1998 there is inserted—

"33A Manual data held by public authorities

(1)   Personal data falling within paragraph (e) of the definition of "data" in section 1(1) are exempt from—
   (a) the first, second, third, fifth, seventh and eighth data protection principles,
   (b) the sixth data protection principle except so far as it relates to the rights conferred on data subjects by sections 7 and 14,
   (c) sections 10 to 12,
   (d) section 13, except so far as it relates to damage caused by a contravention of section 7 or of the fourth data protection principle and to any distress which is also suffered by reason of that contravention,
   (e) Part III, and
   (f) section 55.

(2)   Personal data which fall within paragraph (e) of the definition of "data" in section 1(1) and relate to appointments or removals, pay, discipline, superannuation or other personnel matters, in relation to—
   (a) service in any of the armed forces of the Crown,
   (b) service in any office or employment under the Crown or under any public authority, or
   (c) service in any office or employment, or under any contract for services, in respect of which power to take action, or to determine or approve the action taken, in such matters is

vested in Her Majesty, any Minister of the Crown, the National Assembly for Wales, any Northern Ireland Minister (within the meaning of the Freedom of Information Act 2000) or any public authority,

are also exempt from the remaining data protection principles and the remaining provisions of Part II."

(2) In section 55 of that Act (unlawful obtaining etc of personal data) in subsection (8) after "section 28" there is inserted "or 33A".

(3) In Part III of Schedule 8 to that Act (exemptions available after 23rd October 2001 but before 24th October 2007) after paragraph 14 there is inserted—

"14.—(1) This paragraph applies to personal data which fall within paragraph (e) of the definition of "data" in section 1(1) and do not fall within paragraph 14(1)(a), but does not apply to eligible manual data to which the exemption in paragraph 16 applies.

(2) During the second transitional period, data to which this paragraph applies are exempt from—
(a) the fourth data protection principle, and
(b) section 14(1) to (3)."

(4) In Schedule 13 to that Act (modifications of Act having effect before 24th October 2007) in subsection (4)(b) of section 12A to that Act as set out in paragraph 1, after "paragraph 14" there is inserted "or 14A".

Definitions   For "Northern Ireland Minister", see s 84. For "data", "data subject", "personal data" and "public authority", see the Data Protection Act 1998, s 1(1), as amended (definition "data" amended, definition "public authority" inserted) by s 68(1), (2); for "Minister of the Crown", see s 70(1) of the 1998 Act; for "eligible manual data" and "the second transitional period", see Sch 8, Pt I, para 1 to that Act.

71 Particulars registrable under Part III of Data Protection Act 1998

In section 16(1) of the Data Protection Act 1998 (the registrable particulars), before the word "and" at the end of paragraph (f) there is inserted—

"(ff) where the data controller is a public authority, a statement of that fact,".

Definitions   For "public authority", see the Data Protection Act 1998, s 1(1), as amended by s 69(1), (2); for "data controller", see s 1(1), (4) of that Act.

72 Availability under Act disregarded for purpose of exemption

In section 34 of the Data Protection Act 1998 (information available to the public by or under enactment), after the word "enactment" there is inserted "other than an enactment contained in the Freedom of Information Act 2000".

Other amendments

73 Further amendments of Data Protection Act 1998

Schedule 6 (which contains further amendments of the Data Protection Act 1998) has effect.

PART VIII
MISCELLANEOUS AND SUPPLEMENTAL

74 Power to make provision relating to environmental information

(1)   In this section "the Aarhus Convention" means the Convention on Access to Information, Public Participation in Decision-making and Access to Justice in Environmental Matters signed at Aarhus on 25th June 1998.

(2)   For the purposes of this section "the information provisions" of the Aarhus Convention are Article 4, together with Articles 3 and 9 so far as relating to that Article.

(3)   The Secretary of State may by regulations make such provision as he considers appropriate—

(a)   for the purpose of implementing the information provisions of the Aarhus Convention or any amendment of those provisions made in accordance with Article 14 of the Convention, and

(b)   for the purpose of dealing with matters arising out of or related to the implementation of those provisions or of any such amendment.

(4)   Regulations under subsection (3) may in particular—

(a)   enable charges to be made for making information available in accordance with the regulations,

(b)   provide that any obligation imposed by the regulations in relation to the disclosure of information is to have effect notwithstanding any enactment or rule of law,

(c)   make provision for the issue by the Secretary of State of a code of practice,

(d)   provide for sections 47 and 48 to apply in relation to such a code with such modifications as may be specified,

(e)   provide for any of the provisions of Parts IV and V to apply, with such modifications as may be specified in the regulations, in relation to compliance with any requirement of the regulations, and

(f)   contain such transitional or consequential provision (including provision modifying any enactment) as the Secretary of State considers appropriate.

(5)   This section has effect subject to section 80.

Definitions   For "information", see s 84.
References   See paras 4.75, 4.76, 6.7, 6.8.

75 Power to amend or repeal enactments prohibiting disclosure of information

(1)   If, with respect to any enactment which prohibits the disclosure of information held by a public authority, it appears to the [Lord Chancellor] that by virtue of section 44(1)(a) the enactment is capable of preventing the disclosure of information under section 1, he may by order repeal or amend the enactment for the purpose of removing or relaxing the prohibition.

(2)   In subsection (1)—
"enactment" means—
- (a)   any enactment contained in an Act passed before or in the same Session as this Act, or
- (b)   any enactment contained in Northern Ireland legislation or subordinate legislation passed or made before the passing of this Act;

"information" includes unrecorded information.

(3)   An order under this section may do all or any of the following—
- (a)   make such modifications of enactments as, in the opinion of the [Lord Chancellor], are consequential upon, or incidental to, the amendment or repeal of the enactment containing the prohibition;
- (b)   contain such transitional provisions and savings as appear to the [Lord Chancellor] to be appropriate;
- (c)   make different provision for different cases.

Definitions   For "public authority", see s 3(1); as to "enactment" and for "information" and "subordinate legislation" see s 84.
Amendments: Sub-ss (1), (3): words in square brackets substituted by the Transfer of Functions (Miscellaneous) Order 2001, SI 2001/3500, art 8, Sch 2, para 8(1)(k).
References   See paras 3.6, 6.9.

---

76 Disclosure of information between Commissioner and ombudsmen

(1)   The Commissioner may disclose to a person specified in the first column of the Table below any information obtained by, or furnished to, the Commissioner under or for the purposes of this Act or the Data Protection Act 1998 if it appears to the Commissioner that the information relates to a matter which could be the subject of an investigation by that person under the enactment specified in relation to that person in the second column of that Table.

TABLE

Ombudsman	*Enactment*
The Parliamentary Commissioner for Administration.	The Parliamentary Commissioner Act 1967 (c 13).
The Health Service Commissioner for England.	The Health Service Commissioners Act 1993 (c 46).
The Health Service Commissioner for Wales	The Health Service Commissioners Act 1993 (c 46).
The Health Service Commissioner for Scotland.	The Health Service Commissioners Act 1993 (c 46).
A Local Commissioner as defined by section 23(3) of the Local Government Act 1974.	Part III of the Local Government Act 1974 (c 7).

Ombudsman	Enactment
The Commissioner for Local Administration in Scotland.	Part II of the Local Government (Scotland) Act 1975 (c 30).
The Scottish Parliamentary Commissioner for Administration.	The Scotland Act 1998 (Transitory and Transitional Provisions) (Complaints of Maladministration) Order 1999 (SI 1999/1351).
The Welsh Administration Ombudsman.	Schedule 9 to the Government of Wales Act 1998 (c 38).
The Northern Ireland Commissioner for Complaints	The Commissioner for Complaints (Northern Ireland) Order 1996 (SI 1996/1297 (NI 7)).
The Assembly Ombudsman for Northern Ireland.	The Ombudsman (Northern Ireland) Order 1996 (SI 1996/1298 (NI 8)).

(2) Schedule 7 (which contains amendments relating to information disclosed to ombudsmen under subsection (1) and to the disclosure of information by ombudsmen to the Commissioner) has effect.

Definitions   As to "enactment" and for "the Commissioner" and "information", see s 84.
References   See paras 6.10, 6.11.

77 Offence of altering etc records with intent to prevent disclosure

(1) Where—
  (a) a request for information has been made to a public authority, and
  (b) under section 1 of this Act or section 7 of the Data Protection Act 1998, the applicant would have been entitled (subject to payment of any fee) to communication of any information in accordance with that section,

any person to whom this subsection applies is guilty of an offence if he alters, defaces, blocks, erases, destroys or conceals any record held by the public authority, with the intention of preventing the disclosure by that authority of all, or any part, of the information to the communication of which the applicant would have been entitled.

(2) Subsection (1) applies to the public authority and to any person who is employed by, is an officer of, or is subject to the direction of, the public authority.

(3) A person guilty of an offence under this section is liable on summary conviction to a fine not exceeding level 5 on the standard scale.

(4) No proceedings for an offence under this section shall be instituted—
  (a) in England or Wales, except by the Commissioner or by or with the consent of the Director of Public Prosecutions;
  (b) in Northern Ireland, except by the Commissioner or by or with the consent of the Director of Public Prosecutions for Northern Ireland.

Definitions   For "public authority", see s 3(1); for "request for information", see s 8; for "applicant", "the Commissioner" and "information", see s 84.
References   See paras 3.8, 5.32, 6.11–6.14.

78 Saving for existing powers

Nothing in this Act is to be taken to limit the powers of a public authority to disclose information held by it.

Definitions   For "public authority", see s 3(1); for "information", see s 84.
References   See para 6.15.

79 Defamation

Where any information communicated by a public authority to a person ("the applicant") under section 1 was supplied to the public authority by a third person, the publication to the applicant of any defamatory matter contained in the information shall be privileged unless the publication is shown to have been made with malice.

Definitions   For "public authority", see s 3(1); for "information", see s 84.
References   See para 6.16.

80 Scotland

(1)   No order may be made under section 4(1) or 5 in relation to any of the bodies specified in subsection (2); and the power conferred by section 74(3) does not include power to make provision in relation to information held by any of those bodies.

(2)   The bodies referred to in subsection (1) are—
    (a)   the Scottish Parliament,
    (b)   any part of the Scottish Administration,
    (c)   the Scottish Parliamentary Corporate Body, or
    (d)   any Scottish public authority with mixed functions or no reserved functions (within the meaning of the Scotland Act 1998).

Definitions   For "information", see s 84.

81 Application to government departments, etc

(1)   For the purposes of this Act each government department is to be treated as a person separate from any other government department.

(2)   Subsection (1) does not enable—
    (a)   a government department which is not a Northern Ireland department to claim for the purposes of section 41(1)(b) that the disclosure of any information by it would constitute a breach of confidence actionable by any other government department (not being a Northern Ireland department), or

(b)   a Northern Ireland department to claim for those purposes that the disclosure of information by it would constitute a breach of confidence actionable by any other Northern Ireland department.

(3)   A government department is not liable to prosecution under this Act, but section 77 and paragraph 12 of Schedule 3 apply to a person in the public service of the Crown as they apply to any other person.

(4)   The provisions specified in subsection (3) also apply to a person acting on behalf of either House of Parliament or on behalf of the Northern Ireland Assembly as they apply to any other person.

Definitions   As to "government department" and for "information" and "the Northern Ireland Assembly", see s 84.
References   See paras 5.33, 6.13.

82 Orders and regulations

(1)   Any power of the [Lord Chancellor or the] Secretary of State to make an order or regulations under this Act shall be exercisable by statutory instrument.

(2)   A statutory instrument containing (whether alone or with other provisions)—
    (a)   an order under section 5, 7(3) or (8), 53(1)(a)(iii) or 75, or
    (b)   regulations under section 10(4) or 74(3),
shall not be made unless a draft of the instrument has been laid before, and approved by a resolution of, each House of Parliament.

(3)   A statutory instrument which contains (whether alone or with other provisions)—
    (a)   an order under section 4(1), or
    (b)   regulations under any provision of this Act not specified in subsection (2)(b),
and which is not subject to the requirement in subsection (2) that a draft of the instrument be laid before and approved by a resolution of each House of Parliament, shall be subject to annulment in pursuance of a resolution of either House of Parliament.

(4)   An order under section 4(5) shall be laid before Parliament after being made.

(5)   If a draft of an order under section 5 or 7(8) would, apart from this subsection, be treated for the purposes of the Standing Orders of either House of Parliament as a hybrid instrument, it shall proceed in that House as if it were not such an instrument.

Amendments: Sub-s (1): words in square brackets inserted by the Transfer of Functions (Miscellaneous) Order 2001, SI 2001/3500, art 8, Sch 2, para 8(3).

83 Meaning of "Welsh public authority"

(1)   In this Act "Welsh public authority" means—

    (a)   any public authority which is listed in Part II, III, IV or VI of Schedule 1 and whose functions are exercisable only or mainly in or as regards Wales, other than an excluded authority, or

    (b)   any public authority which is an Assembly subsidiary as defined by section 99(4) of the Government of Wales Act 1998.

(2)   In paragraph (a) of subsection (1) "excluded authority" means a public authority which is designated by the [Lord Chancellor] by order as an excluded authority for the purposes of that paragraph.

(3)   Before making an order under subsection (2), the [Lord Chancellor] shall consult the National Assembly for Wales.

Definitions   For "public authority", see s 3(1).
Amendments: Sub-ss (2), (3): words in square brackets substituted by the Transfer of Functions (Miscellaneous) Order 2001, SI 2001/3500, art 8, Sch 2, para 8(1)(l).

---

84 Interpretation

In this Act, unless the context otherwise requires—

    "applicant", in relation to a request for information, means the person who made the request;

    "appropriate Northern Ireland Minister" means the Northern Ireland Minister in charge of the Department of Culture, Arts and Leisure in Northern Ireland;

    "appropriate records authority", in relation to a transferred public record, has the meaning given by section 15(5);

    "body" includes an unincorporated association;

    "the Commissioner" means the Information Commissioner;

    "decision notice" has the meaning given by section 50;

    "the duty to confirm or deny" has the meaning given by section 1(6);

    "enactment" includes an enactment contained in Northern Ireland legislation;

    "enforcement notice" has the meaning given by section 52;

    "executive committee", in relation to the National Assembly for Wales, has the same meaning as in the Government of Wales Act 1998;

    "exempt information" means information which is exempt information by virtue of any provision of Part II;

    "fees notice" has the meaning given by section 9(1);

    "government department" includes a Northern Ireland department, the Northern Ireland Court Service and any other body or authority exercising statutory functions on behalf of the Crown, but does not include—

        (a)   any of the bodies specified in section 80(2),

        (b)   the Security Service, the Secret Intelligence Service or the Government Communications Headquarters, or

        (c)   the National Assembly for Wales;

    "information" (subject to sections 51(8) and 75(2)) means information recorded in any form;

    "information notice" has the meaning given by section 51;

    "Minister of the Crown" has the same meaning as in the Ministers of the Crown Act 1975;

    "Northern Ireland Minister" includes the First Minister and deputy First Minister in Northern Ireland;

"Northern Ireland public authority" means any public authority, other than the Northern Ireland Assembly or a Northern Ireland department, whose functions are exercisable only or mainly in or as regards Northern Ireland and relate only or mainly to transferred matters;

"prescribed" means prescribed by regulations made by the [Lord Chancellor];

"public authority" has the meaning given by section 3(1);

"public record" means a public record within the meaning of the Public Records Act 1958 or a public record to which the Public Records Act (Northern Ireland) 1923 applies;

"publication scheme" has the meaning given by section 19;

"request for information" has the meaning given by section 8;

"responsible authority", in relation to a transferred public record, has the meaning given by section 15(5);

"the special forces" means those units of the armed forces of the Crown the maintenance of whose capabilities is the responsibility of the Director of Special Forces or which are for the time being subject to the operational command of that Director;

"subordinate legislation" has the meaning given by subsection (1) of section 21 of the Interpretation Act 1978, except that the definition of that term in that subsection shall have effect as if "Act" included Northern Ireland legislation;

"transferred matter", in relation to Northern Ireland, has the meaning given by section 4(1) of the Northern Ireland Act 1998;

"transferred public record" has the meaning given by section 15(4);

"the Tribunal" means the Information Tribunal;

"Welsh public authority" has the meaning given by section 83.

References   See para 3.6.
Amendments: Words in square brackets in definition "prescribed" substituted by the Transfer of Functions (Miscellaneous) Order 2001, SI 2001/3500, art 8, Sch 2, para 8(1)(m).

---

85 Expenses

There shall be paid out of money provided by Parliament—

    (a)   any increase attributable to this Act in the expenses of the [Lord Chancellor] in respect of the Commissioner, the Tribunal or the members of the Tribunal,

    (b)   any administrative expenses of the [Lord Chancellor] attributable to this Act,

    (c)   any other expenses incurred in consequence of this Act by a Minister of the Crown or government department or by either House of Parliament, and

    (d)   any increase attributable to this Act in the sums which under any other Act are payable out of money so provided.

Definitions   As to "government department" and for "the Commissioner", "Minister of the Crown" and "the Tribunal", see s 84.
Amendments: Sub-paras (a), (b): words in square brackets substituted by the Transfer of Functions (Miscellaneous) Order 2001, SI 2001/3500, art 8, Sch 2, para 8(1)(n).

---

86 Repeals

Schedule 8 (repeals) has effect.

87 Commencement

(1)   The following provisions of this Act shall come into force on the day on which this Act is passed—

    (a)   sections 3 to 8 and Schedule 1,

    (b)   section 19 so far as relating to the approval of publication schemes,

    (c)   section 20 so far as relating to the approval and preparation by the Commissioner of model publication schemes,

    (d)   section 47(2) to (6),

    (e)   section 49,

    (f)   section 74,

    (g)   section 75,

    (h)   sections 78 to 85 and this section,

    (i)   paragraphs 2 and 17 to 22 of Schedule 2 (and section 18(4) so far as relating to those paragraphs),

    (j)   paragraph 4 of Schedule 5 (and section 67 so far as relating to that paragraph),

    (k)   paragraph 8 of Schedule 6 (and section 73 so far as relating to that paragraph),

    (l)   Part I of Schedule 8 (and section 86 so far as relating to that Part), and

    (m)   so much of any other provision of this Act as confers power to make any order, regulations or code of practice.

(2)   The following provisions of this Act shall come into force at the end of the period of two months beginning with the day on which this Act is passed—

    (a)   section 18(1),

    (b)   section 76 and Schedule 7,

    (c)   paragraphs 1(1), 3(1), 4, 6, 7, 8(2), 9(2), 10(a), 13(1) and (2), 14(a) and 15(1) and (2) of Schedule 2 (and section 18(4) so far as relating to those provisions), and

    (d)   Part II of Schedule 8 (and section 86 so far as relating to that Part).

(3)   Except as provided by subsections (1) and (2), this Act shall come into force at the end of the period of five years beginning with the day on which this Act is passed or on such day before the end of that period as the [Lord Chancellor] may by order appoint; and different days may be appointed for different purposes.

(4)   An order under subsection (3) may contain such transitional provisions and savings (including provisions capable of having effect after the end of the period referred to in that subsection) as the [Lord Chancellor] considers appropriate.

(5)   During the twelve months beginning with the day on which this Act is passed, and during each subsequent complete period of twelve months in the period beginning with that day and ending with the first day on which all the provisions of this Act are fully in force, the [Lord Chancellor] shall—

    (a)   prepare a report on his proposals for bringing fully into force those provisions of this Act which are not yet fully in force, and

    (b)   lay a copy of the report before each House of Parliament.

Definitions   For "publication scheme", see s 19; for "the Commissioner", see s 84.
Amendments: Sub-ss (3), (4), (5): words in square brackets substituted by the Transfer of Functions (Miscellaneous) Order 2001, SI 2001/3500, art 8, Sch 2, para 8(1)(o).
References   See paras 1.3, 6.17, 6.18.
Orders   The Freedom of Information Act 2000 (Commencement No 1) Order 2001, SI 2001/1637.

88 Short title and extent

(1)   This Act may be cited as the Freedom of Information Act 2000.

(2)   Subject to subsection (3), this Act extends to Northern Ireland.

(3)   The amendment or repeal of any enactment by this Act has the same extent as that enactment.

Definitions   As to "enactment", see s 84.

SCHEDULE 1

Section 3(1)(a)(i)

PUBLIC AUTHORITIES

PART I
GENERAL

1. Any government department.

2. The House of Commons.

3. The House of Lords.

4. The Northern Ireland Assembly.

5. The National Assembly for Wales.

6. The armed forces of the Crown, except—
>   (a)   the special forces, and
>   (b)   any unit or part of a unit which is for the time being required by the Secretary of State to assist the Government Communications Headquarters in the exercise of its functions.

Definitions   For "government department", "the Northern Ireland Assembly" and "the special forces", see s 84.
References   See paras 3.9–3.15, 4.27.

PART II
LOCAL GOVERNMENT

England and Wales

7. A local authority within the meaning of the Local Government Act 1972, namely—
>   (a)   in England, a county council, a London borough council, a district council or a parish council,
>   (b)   in Wales, a county council, a county borough council or a community council.

8. The Greater London Authority.

9. The Common Council of the City of London, in respect of information held in its capacity as a local authority, police authority or port health authority.

10.   The Sub-Treasurer of the Inner Temple or the Under-Treasurer of the Middle Temple, in respect of information held in his capacity as a local authority.

11.   The Council of the Isles of Scilly.

12.   A parish meeting constituted under section 13 of the Local Government Act 1972.

13.   Any charter trustees constituted under section 246 of the Local Government Act 1972.

14.   A fire authority constituted by a combination scheme under section 5 or 6 of the Fire Services Act 1947.

15.   A waste disposal authority established by virtue of an order under section 10(1) of the Local Government Act 1985.

16.   A port health authority constituted by an order under section 2 of the Public Health (Control of Disease) Act 1984.

17.   A licensing planning committee constituted under section 119 of the Licensing Act 1964.

18.   An internal drainage board which is continued in being by virtue of section 1 of the Land Drainage Act 1991.

19.   A joint authority established under Part IV of the Local Government Act 1985 (fire services, civil defence and transport).

20.   The London Fire and Emergency Planning Authority.

21.   A joint fire authority established by virtue of an order under section 42(2) of the Local Government Act 1985 (reorganisation of functions).

22.   A body corporate established pursuant to an order under section 67 of the Local Government Act 1985 (transfer of functions to successors of residuary bodies, etc).

23.   A body corporate established pursuant to an order under section 22 of the Local Government Act 1992 (residuary bodies).

24.   The Broads Authority established by section 1 of the Norfolk and Suffolk Broads Act 1988.

25.   A joint committee constituted in accordance with section 102(1)(b) of the Local Government Act 1972.

26.   A joint board which is continued in being by virtue of section 263(1) of the Local Government Act 1972.

27.   A joint authority established under section 21 of the Local Government Act 1992.

28.   A Passenger Transport Executive for a passenger transport area within the meaning of Part II of the Transport Act 1968.

29.   Transport for London.

30.   The London Transport Users Committee.

31.   A joint board the constituent members of which consist of any of the public authorities described in paragraphs 8, 9, 10, 12, 15, 16, 20 to 31, 57 and 58.

32.   A National Park authority established by an order under section 63 of the Environment Act 1995.

33.   A joint planning board constituted for an area in Wales outside a National Park by an order under section 2(1B) of the Town and Country Planning Act 1990.

34.   A magistrates' court committee established under section 27 of the Justices of the Peace Act 1997.

35.   The London Development Agency.

Northern Ireland

36. A district council within the meaning of the Local Government Act (Northern Ireland) 1972.

Definitions   For "public authority", see s 3(1); for "information", see s 84.
References   See paras 3.9–3.15, 4.27.

PART III
THE NATIONAL HEALTH SERVICE

England and Wales

37. A Health Authority established under section 8 of the National Health Service Act 1977.

38. A special health authority established under section 11 of the National Health Service Act 1977.

39. A primary care trust established under section 16A of the National Health Service Act 1977.

40. A National Health Service trust established under section 5 of the National Health Service and Community Care Act 1990.

41. A Community Health Council established under section 20 of the National Health Service Act 1977.

42. The Dental Practice Board constituted under regulations made under section 37 of the National Health Service Act 1977.

43. The Public Health Laboratory Service Board constituted under Schedule 3 to the National Health Service Act 1977.

44. Any person providing general medical services, general dental services, general ophthalmic services or pharmaceutical services under Part II of the National Health Service Act 1977, in respect of information relating to the provision of those services.

45. Any person providing personal medical services or personal dental services under arrangements made under section 28C of the National Health Service Act 1977, in respect of information relating to the provision of those services.

[45A. Any person providing local pharmaceutical services under—
    (a)   a pilot scheme established under section 28 of the Health and Social Care Act 2001; or
    (b)   an LPS scheme established under Schedule 8A to the National Health Service Act 1977 (c 49),

in respect of information relating to the provision of those services.]

Northern Ireland

46. A Health and Social Services Board established under Article 16 of the Health and Personal Social Services (Northern Ireland) Order 1972.

47. A Health and Social Services Council established under Article 4 of the Health and Personal Social Services (Northern Ireland) Order 1991.

48. A Health and Social Services Trust established under Article 10 of the Health and Personal Social Services (Northern Ireland) Order 1991.

49. A special agency established under Article 3 of the Health and Personal Social Services (Special Agencies) (Northern Ireland) Order 1990.

50. The Northern Ireland Central Services Agency for the Health and Social Services established under Article 26 of the Health and Personal Social Services (Northern Ireland) Order 1972.

51. Any person providing general medical services, general dental services, general ophthalmic services or pharmaceutical services under Part VI of the Health and Personal Social Services (Northern Ireland) Order 1972, in respect of information relating to the provision of those services.

Amendment   Para 45A: inserted by the Health and Social Care Act 2001, s 67(1), Sch 5, Pt I, para 14(1), as from a day to be appointed.
Definitions   For "information" see s 84.
References   See paras 3.9–3.15, 4.27.

PART IV
MAINTAINED SCHOOLS AND OTHER EDUCATIONAL INSTITUTIONS

England and Wales

52.   The governing body of a maintained school, within the meaning of the School Standards and Framework Act 1998.

53.—(1) The governing body of—
  (a)   an institution within the further education sector,
  (b)   a university receiving financial support under section 65 of the Further and Higher Education Act 1992,
  (c)   an institution conducted by a higher education corporation,
  (d)   a designated institution for the purposes of Part II of the Further and Higher Education Act 1992 as defined by section 72(3) of that Act, or
  (e)   any college, school, hall or other institution of a university which falls within paragraph (b).

  (2)   In sub-paragraph (1)—
  (a)   "governing body" is to be interpreted in accordance with subsection (1) of section 90 of the Further and Higher Education Act 1992 but without regard to subsection (2) of that section,
  (b)   in paragraph (a), the reference to an institution within the further education sector is to be construed in accordance with section 91(3) of the Further and Higher Education Act 1992,
  (c)   in paragraph (c), "higher education corporation" has the meaning given by section 90(1) of that Act, and
  (d)   in paragraph (e) "college" includes any institution in the nature of a college.

Northern Ireland

54.—(1) The managers of—
  (a)   a controlled school, voluntary school or grant-maintained integrated school within the meaning of Article 2(2) of the Education and Libraries (Northern Ireland) Order 1986, or
  (b)   a pupil referral unit as defined by Article 87(1) of the Education (Northern Ireland) Order 1998.

  (2)   In sub-paragraph (1) "managers" has the meaning given by Article 2(2) of the Education and Libraries (Northern Ireland) Order 1986.

55.—(1) The governing body of—
  (a)   a university receiving financial support under Article 30 of the Education and Libraries (Northern Ireland) Order 1993,
  (b)   a college of education maintained in pursuance of arrangements under Article 66(1) or in respect of which grants are paid under Article 66(2) or (3) of the Education and Libraries (Northern Ireland) Order 1986, or
  (c)   an institution of further education within the meaning of the Further Education (Northern Ireland) Order 1997.

  (2)   In sub-paragraph (1) "governing body" has the meaning given by Article 30(3) of the Education and Libraries (Northern Ireland) Order 1993.

56. Any person providing further education to whom grants, loans or other payments are made under Article 5(1)(b) of the Further Education (Northern Ireland) Order 1997.

References   See paras 3.9–3.15, 4.27.

PART V
POLICE

England and Wales

57. A police authority established under section 3 of the Police Act 1996.

58. The Metropolitan Police Authority established under section 5B of the Police Act 1996.

59. A chief officer of police of a police force in England or Wales.

Northern Ireland

60. The *Police Authority for Northern Ireland.*

61. The Chief Constable of the *Royal Ulster Constabulary.*

Miscellaneous

62. The British Transport Police.

63. The Ministry of Defence Police established by section 1 of the Ministry of Defence Police Act 1987.

64. Any person who—
    (a) by virtue of any enactment has the function of nominating individuals who may be appointed as special constables by justices of the peace, and
    (b) is not a public authority by virtue of any other provision of this Act,

in respect of information relating to the exercise by any person appointed on his nomination of the functions of a special constable.

Amendment In para 60, for the words in italics there are substituted the words "Northern Ireland Policing Board" and in para 61 for the words in italics there are substituted the words "Police Service of Northern Ireland" by the Police (Northern Ireland) Act 2000, s 78(1), Sch 6, para 25(1), (2), as from a day to be appointed.
Definitions For "public authority", see s 3(1); as to "enactment" and for "information", see s 84.
References See paras 3.9–3.15, 4.27.

PART VI
OTHER PUBLIC BODIES AND OFFICES: GENERAL

The Adjudicator for the Inland Revenue and Customs and Excise.
The Administration of Radioactive Substances Advisory Committee.
The Advisory Board on Family Law.
The Advisory Board on Restricted Patients.
The Advisory Board on the Registration of Homoeopathic Products.
The Advisory Committee for Cleaner Coal Technology.
The Advisory Committee for Disabled People in Employment and Training.
The Advisory Committee for the Public Lending Right.
The Advisory Committee for Wales (in relation to the Environment Agency).
The Advisory Committee on Advertising.
The Advisory Committee on Animal Feedingstuffs.
The Advisory Committee on Borderline Substances.
The Advisory Committee on Business and the Environment.
The Advisory Committee on Business Appointments.
The Advisory Committee on Conscientious Objectors.
The Advisory Committee on Consumer Products and the Environment.
The Advisory Committee on Dangerous Pathogens.

The Advisory Committee on Distinction Awards.

An Advisory Committee on General Commissioners of Income Tax.

The Advisory Committee on the Government Art Collection.

The Advisory Committee on Hazardous Substances.

The Advisory Committee on Historic Wreck Sites.

An Advisory Committee on Justices of the Peace in England and Wales.

The Advisory Committee on the Microbiological Safety of Food.

The Advisory Committee on NHS Drugs.

The Advisory Committee on Novel Foods and Processes.

The Advisory Committee on Overseas Economic and Social Research.

The Advisory Committee on Packaging.

The Advisory Committee on Pesticides.

The Advisory Committee on Releases to the Environment.

The Advisory Council on Libraries.

The Advisory Council on the Misuse of Drugs.

The Advisory Council on Public Records.

The Advisory Group on Hepatitis.

The Advisory Panel on Standards for the Planning Inspectorate.

The Aerospace Committee.

An Agricultural Dwelling House Advisory Committee.

An Agricultural Wages Board for England and Wales.

An Agricultural Wages Committee.

The Agriculture and Environment Biotechnology Commission.

The Airborne Particles Expert Group.

The Alcohol Education and Research Council.

The Ancient Monuments Board for Wales.

The Animal Procedures Committee.

The Animal Welfare Advisory Committee.

The Apple and Pear Research Council.

The Armed Forces Pay Review Body.

The Arts Council of England.

The Arts Council of Wales.

The Audit Commission for Local Authorities and the National Health Service in England and Wales.

The Auditor General for Wales.

The Authorised Conveyancing Practitioners Board.

The Bank of England, in respect of information held for purposes other than those of its functions with respect to—
    (a)   monetary policy,
    (b)   financial operations intended to support financial institutions for the purposes of maintaining stability, and
    (c)   the provision of private banking services and related services.

The Better Regulation Task Force.

The Biotechnology and Biological Sciences Research Council.

Any Board of Visitors established under section 6(2) of the Prison Act 1952.

The Britain-Russia Centre and East-West Centre.

The British Association for Central and Eastern Europe.

The British Broadcasting Corporation, in respect of information held for purposes other than those of journalism, art or literature.

The British Coal Corporation.

The British Council.

The British Educational Communications and Technology Agency.

The British Hallmarking Council.

The British Library.
The British Museum.
The British Pharmacopoeia Commission.
The British Potato Council.
The British Railways Board.
British Shipbuilders.
The British Tourist Authority.
The British Waterways Board.
The British Wool Marketing Board.
The Broadcasting Standards Commission.
The Building Regulations Advisory Committee.
The Central Advisory Committee on War Pensions.
The Central Council for Education and Training in Social Work (UK).
[The Central Police Training and Development Authority.]
The Central Rail Users' Consultative Committee.
The Channel Four Television Corporation, in respect of information held for purposes other than those of journalism, art or literature.
The Children and Family Court Advisory and Support Service.
The Civil Aviation Authority.
The Civil Justice Council.
The Civil Procedure Rule Committee.
The Civil Service Appeal Board.
The Civil Service Commissioners.
The Coal Authority.
The Commission for Architecture and the Built Environment.
The Commission for Health Improvement.
The Commission for Local Administration in England.
The Commission for Local Administration in Wales.
The Commission for Racial Equality.
The Commission for the New Towns.
The Commissioner for Integrated Transport.
The Commissioner for Public Appointments.
The Committee for Monitoring Agreements on Tobacco Advertising and Sponsorship.
The Committee of Investigation for Great Britain.
The Committee on Agricultural Valuation.
The Committee on Carcinogenicity of Chemicals in Food, Consumer Products and the Environment.
The Committee on Chemicals and Materials of Construction For Use in Public Water Supply and Swimming Pools.
The Committee on Medical Aspects of Food and Nutrition Policy.
The Committee on Medical Aspects of Radiation in the Environment.
The Committee on Mutagenicity of Chemicals in Food, Consumer Products and the Environment.
The Committee on Standards in Public Life.
The Committee on Toxicity of Chemicals in Food, Consumer Products and the Environment.
The Committee on the Medical Effects of Air Pollutants.
The Committee on the Safety of Medicines.
The Commonwealth Scholarship Commission in the United Kingdom.
The Community Development Foundation.
The Competition Commission, in relation to information held by it otherwise than as a tribunal.
The Construction Industry Training Board.

Consumer Communications for England.

The Consumer Panel.

The consumers' committee for Great Britain appointed under section 19 of the Agricultural Marketing Act 1958.

The Council for Professions Supplementary to Medicine.

The Council for the Central Laboratory of the Research Councils.

The Council for Science and Technology.

The Council on Tribunals.

The Countryside Agency.

The Countryside Council for Wales.

The Covent Garden Market Authority.

The Criminal Cases Review Commission.

The Criminal Justice Consultative Council.

The Crown Court Rule Committee.

The Dartmoor Steering Group and Working Party.

The Darwin Advisory Committee.

The Defence Nuclear Safety Committee.

The Defence Scientific Advisory Council.

The Design Council.

The Development Awareness Working Group.

The Diplomatic Service Appeal Board.

The Disability Living Allowance Advisory Board.

The Disability Rights Commission.

The Disabled Persons Transport Advisory Committee.

The Economic and Social Research Council.

The Education Transfer Council.

The Energy Advisory Panel.

The Engineering Construction Industry Training Board.

The Engineering and Physical Sciences Research Council.

The English National Board for Nursing, Midwifery and Health Visiting.

English Nature.

The English Sports Council.

The English Tourist Board.

The Environment Agency.

The Equal Opportunities Commission.

The Expert Advisory Group on AIDS.

The Expert Group on Cryptosporidium in Water Supplies.

An Expert Panel on Air Quality Standards.

The Export Guarantees Advisory Council.

The Family Proceedings Rules Committee.

The Farm Animal Welfare Council.

The Fire Services Examination Board.

The Firearms Consultative Committee.

The Food Advisory Committee.

Food from Britain.

The Football Licensing Authority.

The Fuel Cell Advisory Panel.

The Further Education Funding Council for Wales.

The Gaming Board for Great Britain.

The Gas Consumers' Council.

The Gene Therapy Advisory Committee.

The General Chiropractic Council.

The General Dental Council.

The General Medical Council.
The General Osteopathic Council.
The Genetic Testing and Insurance Committee.
The Government Hospitality Advisory Committee for the Purchase of Wine.
The Government Chemist.
The Great Britain-China Centre.
The Health and Safety Commission.
The Health and Safety Executive.
The Health Service Commissioner for England.
The Health Service Commissioner for Wales.
[Her Majesty's Chief Inspector of Education and Training in Wales or Prif Arolygydd Ei
    Mawrhydi dros Addysg a Hyfforddiant yng Nghymru.]
The Higher Education Funding Council for England.
The Higher Education Funding Council for Wales.
The Hill Farming Advisory Committee.
The Hill Farming Advisory Sub-committee for Wales.
The Historic Buildings Council for Wales.
The Historic Buildings and Monuments Commission for England.
The Historic Royal Palaces Trust.
The Home-Grown Cereals Authority.
The Honorary Investment Advisory Committee.
The Horserace Betting Levy Board.
The Horserace Totalisator Board.
The Horticultural Development Council.
Horticulture Research International.
The House of Lords Appointments Commission.
Any housing action trust established under Part III of the Housing Act 1988.
The Housing Corporation.
The Human Fertilisation and Embryology Authority.
The Human Genetics Commission.
The Immigration Services Commissioner.
The Imperial War Museum.
The Independent Board of Visitors for Military Corrective Training Centres.
The Independent Case Examiner for the Child Support Agency.
The Independent Living Funds.
The Independent Television Commission.
The Indian Family Pensions Funds Body of Commissioners.
The Industrial Development Advisory Board.
The Industrial Injuries Advisory Council.
The Information Commissioner.
The Inland Waterways Amenity Advisory Council.
The Insolvency Rules Committee.
. . .
Investors in People UK.
The Joint Committee on Vaccination and Immunisation.
The Joint Nature Conservation Committee.
The Joint Prison/Probation Accreditation Panel.
The Judicial Studies Board.
The Know-How Fund Advisory Board.
The Land Registration Rule Committee.
The Law Commission.
The Legal Services Commission.
The Legal Services Consultative Panel.

The Legal Services Ombudsman.
The Library and Information Services Council (Wales).
The Local Government Boundary Commission for Wales.
The Local Government Commission for England.
A local probation board established under section 4 of the Criminal Justice and Court Services Act 2000.
The London Pensions Fund Authority.
The Low Pay Commission.
The Magistrates' Courts Rules Committee.
The Marshall Aid Commemoration Commission.
The Measurement Advisory Committee.
The Meat and Livestock Commission.
The Medical Practices Committee.
The Medical Research Council.
The Medical Workforce Standing Advisory Committee.
The Medicines Commission.
The Milk Development Council.
The Millennium Commission.
The Museum of London.
The National Army Museum.
The National Audit Office.
The National Biological Standards Board (UK).
The National Consumer Council.
The National Crime Squad.
The National Employers' Liaison Committee.
The National Endowment for Science, Technology and the Arts.
The National Expert Group on Transboundary Air Pollution.
The National Gallery.
The National Heritage Memorial Fund.
The National Library of Wales
The National Lottery Charities Board.
The National Lottery Commission.
The National Maritime Museum.
The National Museum of Science and Industry.
The National Museums and Galleries of Wales.
The National Museums and Galleries on Merseyside.
The National Portrait Gallery.
The National Radiological Protection Board.
The Natural Environment Research Council.
The Natural History Museum.
The New Deal Task Force.
The New Opportunities Fund.
The Occupational Pensions Regulatory Authority.
The Oil and Pipelines Agency.
The OSO Board.
The Overseas Service Pensions Scheme Advisory Board.
The Panel on Standards for the Planning Inspectorate.
The Parliamentary Boundary Commission for England.
The Parliamentary Boundary Commission for Scotland.
The Parliamentary Boundary Commission for Wales.
The Parliamentary Commissioner for Administration.
The Parole Board.
The Particle Physics and Astronomy Research Council.

[The Patient Information Advisory Group.]
The Pensions Compensation Board.
The Pensions Ombudsman.
The Pharmacists' Review Panel.
The Place Names Advisory Committee.
The Poisons Board.
The Police Complaints Authority.
The Police Information Technology Organisation.
The Police Negotiating Board.
The Political Honours Scrutiny Committee.
The Post Office.
The Post Office Users' Councils for Scotland, Wales and Northern Ireland.
The Post Office Users' National Council.
The Property Advisory Group.
The Qualifications, Curriculum and Assessment Authority for Wales.
The Qualifications Curriculum Authority.
The Race Education and Employment Forum.
The Race Relations Forum.
The Radio Authority.
The Radioactive Waste Management Advisory Committee.
A Regional Cultural Consortium.
Any regional development agency established under the Regional Development Agencies Act 1998, other than the London Development Agency.
Any regional flood defence committee.
The Registrar of Occupational and Personal Pension Schemes.
The Registrar of Public Lending Right.
Remploy Ltd.
The Renewable Energy Advisory Committee.
Resource: The Council for Museums, Archives and Libraries.
The Review Board for Government Contracts.
The Review Body for Nursing Staff, Midwives, Health Visitors and Professions Allied to Medicine.
The Review Body on Doctors and Dentists Remuneration.
The Reviewing Committee on the Export of Works of Art.
The Royal Air Force Museum.
The Royal Armouries.
The Royal Botanic Gardens, Kew.
The Royal Commission on Ancient and Historical Monuments of Wales.
The Royal Commission on Environmental Pollution.
The Royal Commission on Historical Manuscripts.
The Royal Military College of Science Advisory Council.
The Royal Mint Advisory Committee on the Design of Coins, Medals, Seals and Decorations.
The School Teachers' Review Body.
The Scientific Committee on Tobacco and Health.
The Scottish Advisory Committee on Telecommunications.
The Scottish Committee of the Council on Tribunals.
The Sea Fish Industry Authority.
[The Security Industry Authority.]
The Senior Salaries Review Body.
The Sentencing Advisory Panel.
The Service Authority for the National Crime Squad.

Sianel Pedwar Cymru, in respect of information held for purposes other than those of journalism, art or literature.

Sir John Soane's Museum.

The Skills Task Force.

The social fund Commissioner appointed under section 65 of the Social Security Administration Act 1992.

The Social Security Advisory Committee.

The Social Services Inspectorate for Wales Advisory Group.

The Spongiform Encephalopathy Advisory Committee.

The Sports Council for Wales.

The Standing Advisory Committee on Industrial Property.

The Standing Advisory Committee on Trunk Road Assessment.

The Standing Dental Advisory Committee.

The Standing Nursing and Midwifery Advisory Committee.

The Standing Medical Advisory Committee.

The Standing Pharmaceutical Advisory Committee.

The Steering Committee on Pharmacy Postgraduate Education.

[Strategic Rail Authority.]

The subsidence adviser appointed under section 46 of the Coal Industry Act 1994.

The Substance Misuse Advisory Panel.

The Sustainable Development Commission.

The Sustainable Development Education Panel.

The Tate Gallery.

The Teacher Training Agency.

The Theatres Trust.

The Traffic Commissioners, in respect of information held by them otherwise than as a tribunal.

The Treasure Valuation Committee.

The UK Advisory Panel for Health Care Workers Infected with Bloodborne Viruses.

The UK Sports Council.

The United Kingdom Atomic Energy Authority.

The United Kingdom Central Council for Nursing, Midwifery and Health Visiting.

The United Kingdom Register of Organic Food Standards.

The United Kingdom Xenotransplantation Interim Regulatory Authority.

The Unlinked Anonymous Serosurveys Steering Group.

The Unrelated Live Transplant Regulatory Authority.

The Urban Regeneration Agency.

The Veterinary Products Committee.

The Victoria and Albert Museum.

The Wales New Deal Advisory Task Force.

The Wales Tourist Board.

The Wallace Collection.

The War Pensions Committees.

The Water Regulations Advisory Committee.

The Welsh Administration Ombudsman.

The Welsh Advisory Committee on Telecommunications.

The Welsh Committee for Professional Development of Pharmacy.

The Welsh Dental Committee.

The Welsh Development Agency.

The Welsh Industrial Development Advisory Board.

The Welsh Language Board.

The Welsh Medical Committee.

The Welsh National Board for Nursing, Midwifery and Health Visiting.

The Welsh Nursing and Midwifery Committee.
The Welsh Optometric Committee.
The Welsh Pharmaceutical Committee.
The Welsh Scientific Advisory Committee.
The Westminster Foundation for Democracy.
The Wilton Park Academic Council.
The Wine Standards Board of the Vintners' Company.
The Women's National Commission.
The Youth Justice Board for England and Wales.
The Zoos Forum.

Amendment Entry "The British Railways Board" repealed and entry "Strategic Rail Authority" inserted by the Transport Act 2000, ss 204, 274, Sch 14, Pt V, para 30, Sch 31, Pt IV, as from a day to be appointed; entry "The Central Police Training and Development Authority" inserted by the Criminal Justice and Police Act 2001, s 102, Sch 4, para 8, as from a day to be appointed; entry "Her Majesty's Chief Inspector of Education and Training in Wales or Prif Arolygydd Ei Mawrhydi dros Addysg a Hyfforddiant yng Nghymru" substituted by the Learning and Skills Act 2000, s 73(1), (3)(a); entry "The Insurance Brokers Registration Council" (omitted) repealed by the Financial Services and Markets Act 2000 (Dissolution of the Insurance Brokers Registration Council) (Consequential Provisions) Order 2001, SI 2001/1283, art 3(7); entry "The Patient Information Advisory Group." inserted by the Health and Social Care Act 2001, s 67(1), Sch 5, Pt 3, para 18; entry "The Security Industry Authority" inserted by the Private Security Industry Act 2001, s 1, Sch 1, para 23, as from a day to be appointed.
References See paras 3.9–3.15, 4.27.

PART VII
OTHER PUBLIC BODIES AND OFFICES: NORTHERN IRELAND

An Advisory Committee on General Commissioners of Income Tax (Northern Ireland).
The Advisory Committee on Justices of the Peace in Northern Ireland.
The Advisory Committee on Juvenile Court Lay Panel (Northern Ireland).
The Advisory Committee on Pesticides for Northern Ireland.
The Agricultural Research Institute of Northern Ireland.
The Agricultural Wages Board for Northern Ireland.
The Arts Council of Northern Ireland.
The Assembly Ombudsman for Northern Ireland.
The Board of Trustees of National Museums and Galleries of Northern Ireland.
Boards of Visitors and Visiting Committees.
The Boundary Commission for Northern Ireland.
The Charities Advisory Committee.
The Chief Electoral Officer for Northern Ireland.
The Civil Service Commissioners for Northern Ireland.
The Commissioner for Public Appointments for Northern Ireland.
The Construction Industry Training Board.
The consultative Civic Forum referred to in section 56(4) of the Northern Ireland Act 1998.
The Council for Catholic Maintained Schools.
The Council for Nature Conservation and the Countryside.
The County Court Rules Committee (Northern Ireland).
The Disability Living Allowance Advisory Board for Northern Ireland.
The Distinction and Meritorious Service Awards Committee.
[A district policing partnership.]
The Drainage Council for Northern Ireland.
An Education and Library Board established under Article 3 of the Education and Libraries (Northern Ireland) Order 1986.

Enterprise Ulster.
The Equality Commission for Northern Ireland.
The Family Proceedings Rules Committee (Northern Ireland).
The Fire Authority for Northern Ireland.
The Fisheries Conservancy Board for Northern Ireland.
The General Consumer Council for Northern Ireland.
The Health and Safety Agency for Northern Ireland.
The Historic Buildings Council.
The Historic Monuments Council.
The Independent Assessor of Military Complaints Procedures in Northern Ireland.
The Independent Reviewer of the Northern Ireland (Emergency Provisions) Act.
The Independent Commissioner for Holding Centres.
The Industrial Development Board for Northern Ireland.
The Industrial Research and Technology Unit.
The Juvenile Justice Board.
The Labour Relations Agency.
The Laganside Corporation.
The Law Reform Advisory Committee for Northern Ireland.
The Lay Observer for Northern Ireland.
The Legal Aid Advisory Committee (Northern Ireland).
[The Life Sentence Review Commissioners appointed under Article 3 of the Life
    Sentences (Northern Ireland) Order 2001.]
The Livestock & Meat Commission for Northern Ireland.
The Local Enterprise Development Unit.
The Local Government Staff Commission.
The Magistrates' Courts Rules Committee (Northern Ireland).
The Mental Health Commission for Northern Ireland.
The Northern Ireland Advisory Committee on Telecommunications.
The Northern Ireland Audit Office.
The Northern Ireland Building Regulations Advisory Committee.
The Northern Ireland Civil Service Appeal Board.
The Northern Ireland Commissioner for Complaints.
The Northern Ireland Community Relations Council.
The Northern Ireland Consumer Committee for Electricity.
The Northern Ireland Council for the Curriculum, Examinations and Assessment.
The Northern Ireland Council for Postgraduate Medical and Dental Education.
The Northern Ireland Crown Court Rules Committee.
The Northern Ireland Economic Council.
The Northern Ireland Fishery Harbour Authority.
The Northern Ireland Higher Education Council.
The Northern Ireland Housing Executive.
The Northern Ireland Human Rights Commission.
The Northern Ireland Insolvency Rules Committee.
The Northern Ireland Local Government Officers' Superannuation Committee.
The Northern Ireland Museums Council.
The Northern Ireland Pig Production Development Committee.
The Northern Ireland Supreme Court Rules Committee.
The Northern Ireland Tourist Board.
The Northern Ireland Transport Holding Company.
The Northern Ireland Water Council.
The Parades Commission.
The Police Ombudsman for Northern Ireland.
The Probation Board for Northern Ireland.

The Rural Development Council for Northern Ireland.

The Sentence Review Commissioners appointed under section 1 of the Northern Ireland (Sentences) Act 1998.

The social fund Commissioner appointed under Article 37 of the Social Security (Northern Ireland) Order 1998.

The Sports Council for Northern Ireland.

The Staff Commission for Education and Library Boards.

The Statistics Advisory Committee.

The Statute Law Committee for Northern Ireland.

The Training and Employment Agency.

Ulster Supported Employment Ltd.

The Youth Council for Northern Ireland.

Amendment Entry "A district policing partnership" inserted by the Police (Northern Ireland) Act 2000, s 78(1), Sch 6, para 25(1), (3), as from a day to be appointed; entry "The Life Sentence Review Commissioners appointed under Article 3 of the Life Sentences (Northern Ireland) Order 2001" inserted by the Life Sentences (Northern Ireland) Order 2001, SI 2001/2565, art 4, as from a day to be appointed.
References   See paras 3.9–3.15, 4.27.

Section 18(4)

SCHEDULE 2

THE COMMISSIONER AND THE TRIBUNAL

PART I
PROVISION CONSEQUENTIAL ON S 18(1) AND (2)

General

1.—(1)   Any reference in any enactment, instrument or document to the Data Protection Commissioner or the Data Protection Registrar shall be construed, in relation to any time after the commencement of section 18(1), as a reference to the Information Commissioner.

(2)   Any reference in any enactment, instrument or document to the Data Protection Tribunal shall be construed, in relation to any time after the commencement of section 18(2), as a reference to the Information Tribunal.

2.—(1)   Any reference in this Act or in any instrument under this Act to the Commissioner shall be construed, in relation to any time before the commencement of section 18(1), as a reference to the Data Protection Commissioner.

(2)   Any reference in this Act or in any instrument under this Act to the Tribunal shall be construed, in relation to any time before the commencement of section 18(2), as a reference to the Data Protection Tribunal.

Public Records Act 1958 (c 51)

3.—(1)   In Part II of the Table in paragraph 3 of Schedule 1 to the Public Records Act 1958 (definition of public records), the entry relating to the Data Protection Commissioner is omitted and there is inserted at the appropriate place—

"Information Commissioner."

(2)   In paragraph 4(1) of that Schedule, for paragraph (nn) there is substituted—

"(nn) records of the Information Tribunal;".

Parliamentary Commissioner Act 1967 (c 13)

4. In Schedule 2 to the Parliamentary Commissioner Act 1967 (departments etc subject to investigation), the entry relating to the Data Protection Commissioner is omitted and there is inserted at the appropriate place—

"Information Commissioner".

5. In Schedule 4 to that Act (tribunals exercising administrative functions), for the entry relating to the Data Protection Tribunal there is substituted—

"Information Tribunal constituted under section 6 of the Data Protection Act 1998."

Superannuation Act 1972 (c 11)

6. In Schedule 1 to the Superannuation Act 1972 (employment with superannuation scheme), for "Data Protection Commissioner" there is substituted "Information Commissioner".

Consumer Credit Act 1974 (c 39)

7. In section 159 of the Consumer Credit Act 1974 (correction of wrong information), in subsections (7) and (8)(b), for "Data Protection Commissioner", in both places where it occurs, there is substituted "Information Commissioner".

House of Commons Disqualification Act 1975 (c 24)

8.—(1) In Part II of Schedule 1 to the House of Commons Disqualification Act 1975 (bodies whose members are disqualified), the entry relating to the Data Protection Tribunal is omitted and there is inserted at the appropriate place—

"The Information Tribunal".

(2) In Part III of that Schedule (disqualifying offices), the entry relating to the Data Protection Commissioner is omitted and there is inserted at the appropriate place—

"The Information Commissioner".

Northern Ireland Assembly Disqualification Act 1975 (c 25)

9.—(1) In Part II of Schedule 1 to the Northern Ireland Assembly Disqualification Act 1975 (bodies whose members are disqualified), the entry relating to the Data Protection Tribunal is omitted and there is inserted at the appropriate place—

"The Information Tribunal".

(2) In Part III of that Schedule (disqualifying offices), the entry relating to the Data Protection Commissioner is omitted and there is inserted at the appropriate place—

"The Information Commissioner".

Tribunals and Inquiries Act 1992 (c 53)

10. In paragraph 14 of Part I of Schedule 1 to the Tribunals and Inquiries Act 1992 (tribunals under direct supervision of Council on Tribunals)—
    (a)   in sub-paragraph (a), for "The Data Protection Commissioner" there is substituted "The Information Commissioner", and
    (b)   for sub-paragraph (b) there is substituted—

"(b) the Information Tribunal constituted under that section, in respect of its jurisdiction under—
    (i)   section 48 of that Act, and
    (ii)   section 57 of the Freedom of Information Act 2000."

Judicial Pensions and Retirement Act 1993 (c 8)

11. In Schedule 5 to the Judicial Pensions and Retirement Act 1993 (retirement provisions: the relevant offices), in the entry relating to the chairman and deputy chairman of the Data Protection Tribunal, for "the Data Protection Tribunal" there is substituted "the Information Tribunal".

12. In Schedule 7 to that Act (retirement dates: transitional provisions), in paragraph 5(5)(xxvi) for "the Data Protection Tribunal" there is substituted "the Information Tribunal".

Data Protection Act 1998 (c 29)

13.—(1) Section 6 of the Data Protection Act 1998 (the Data Protection Commissioner and the Data Protection Tribunal) is amended as follows.

    (2)   For subsection (1) there is substituted—

> "(1) For the purposes of this Act and of the Freedom of Information Act 2000 there shall be an officer known as the Information Commissioner (in this Act referred to as "the Commissioner")."

    (3)   For subsection (3) there is substituted—

> "(3) For the purposes of this Act and of the Freedom of Information Act 2000 there shall be a tribunal known as the Information Tribunal (in this Act referred to as "the Tribunal")."

14. In section 70(1) of that Act (supplementary definitions)—

        (a)   in the definition of "the Commissioner", for "the Data Protection Commissioner" there is substituted "the Information Commissioner", and

        (b)   in the definition of "the Tribunal", for "the Data Protection Tribunal" there is substituted "the Information Tribunal".

15.—(1) Schedule 5 to that Act (the Data Protection Commissioner and the Data Protection Tribunal) is amended as follows.

    (2)   In paragraph 1(1), for "Data Protection Commissioner" there is substituted "Information Commissioner".

    (3)   Part III shall cease to have effect.

Definitions   As to "enactment" and for "the Commissioner" and "the Tribunal", see s 84.

PART II
AMENDMENTS RELATING TO EXTENSION OF FUNCTIONS OF COMMISSIONER AND TRIBUNAL

Interests represented by lay members of Tribunal

16. In section 6(6) of the Data Protection Act 1998 (lay members of Tribunal)—

        (a)   for the word "and" at the end of paragraph (a) there is substituted—

> "(aa) persons to represent the interests of those who make requests for information under the Freedom of Information Act 2000,", and

        (b)   after paragraph (b) there is inserted

> "and
> (bb) persons to represent the interests of public authorities."

Expenses incurred under this Act excluded in calculating fees

17. In section 26(2) of that Act (fees regulations), in paragraph (a)—

        (a)   after "functions" there is inserted "under this Act", and

        (b)   after "Tribunal" there is inserted "so far as attributable to their functions under this Act".

Information provided to Commissioner or Tribunal

18. In section 58 of that Act (disclosure of information to Commissioner or Tribunal), after "this Act" there is inserted "or the Freedom of Information Act 2000".

19.—(1) Section 59 of that Act (confidentiality of information) is amended as follows.

(2) In subsections (1) and (2), for "this Act", wherever occurring, there is substituted "the information Acts".

(3) After subsection (3) there is inserted—

"(4) In this section "the information Acts" means this Act and the Freedom of Information Act 2000."

Deputy commissioners

20.—(1) Paragraph 4 of Schedule 5 to that Act (officers and staff) is amended as follows.

(2) In sub-paragraph (1)(a), after "a deputy commissioner" there is inserted "or two deputy commissioners".

(3) After sub-paragraph (1) there is inserted—

"(1A)The Commissioner shall, when appointing any second deputy commissioner, specify which of the Commissioner's functions are to be performed, in the circumstances referred to in paragraph 5(1), by each of the deputy commissioners."

Exercise of Commissioner's functions by others

21.—(1) Paragraph 5 of Schedule 5 to that Act (exercise of functions of Commissioner during vacancy etc) is amended as follows.

(2) In sub-paragraph (1)—
    (a) after "deputy commissioner" there is inserted "or deputy commissioners", and
    (b) after "this Act" there is inserted "or the Freedom of Information Act 2000".

(3) In sub-paragraph (2) after "this Act" there is inserted "or the Freedom of Information Act 2000".

Money

22. In paragraph 9(1) of Schedule 5 to that Act (money) for "or section 159 of the Consumer Credit Act 1974" there is substituted ", under section 159 of the Consumer Credit Act 1974 or under the Freedom of Information Act 2000".

Definitions   As to "the Commissioner" and "the Tribunal", see s 84.

SCHEDULE 3

Section 55

POWERS OF ENTRY AND INSPECTION

Issue of warrants

1.—(1) If a circuit judge is satisfied by information on oath supplied by the Commissioner that there are reasonable grounds for suspecting—
    (a) that a public authority has failed or is failing to comply with—
        (i) any of the requirements of Part I of this Act,
        (ii) so much of a decision notice as requires steps to be taken, or
        (iii) an information notice or an enforcement notice, or
    (b) that an offence under section 77 has been or is being committed,

and that evidence of such a failure to comply or of the commission of the offence is to be found on any premises specified in the information, he may, subject to paragraph 2, grant a warrant to the Commissioner.

(2)　A warrant issued under sub-paragraph (1) shall authorise the Commissioner or any of his officers or staff at any time within seven days of the date of the warrant—

    (a)　to enter and search the premises,

    (b)　to inspect and seize any documents or other material found there which may be such evidence as is mentioned in that sub-paragraph, and

    (c)　to inspect, examine, operate and test any equipment found there in which information held by the public authority may be recorded.

2.—(1)　A judge shall not issue a warrant under this Schedule unless he is satisfied—

    (a)　that the Commissioner has given seven days' notice in writing to the occupier of the premises in question demanding access to the premises, and

    (b)　that either—

        (i)　access was demanded at a reasonable hour and was unreasonably refused, or

        (ii)　although entry to the premises was granted, the occupier unreasonably refused to comply with a request by the Commissioner or any of the Commissioner's officers or staff to permit the Commissioner or the officer or member of staff to do any of the things referred to in paragraph 1(2), and

    (c)　that the occupier, has, after the refusal, been notified by the Commissioner of the application for the warrant and has had an opportunity of being heard by the judge on the question whether or not it should be issued.

(2)　Sub-paragraph (1) shall not apply if the judge is satisfied that the case is one of urgency or that compliance with those provisions would defeat the object of the entry.

3.　A judge who issues a warrant under this Schedule shall also issue two copies of it and certify them clearly as copies.

Execution of warrants

4.　A person executing a warrant issued under this Schedule may use such reasonable force as may be necessary.

5.　A warrant issued under this Schedule shall be executed at a reasonable hour unless it appears to the person executing it that there are grounds for suspecting that the evidence in question would not be found if it were so executed.

6.—(1)　If the premises in respect of which a warrant is issued under this Schedule are occupied by a public authority and any officer or employee of the authority is present when the warrant is executed, he shall be shown the warrant and supplied with a copy of it; and if no such officer or employee is present a copy of the warrant shall be left in a prominent place on the premises.

(2)　If the premises in respect of which a warrant is issued under this Schedule are occupied by a person other than a public authority and he is present when the warrant is executed, he shall be shown the warrant and supplied with a copy of it; and if that person is not present a copy of the warrant shall be left in a prominent place on the premises.

7.—(1)　A person seizing anything in pursuance of a warrant under this Schedule shall give a receipt for it if asked to do so.

(2)　Anything so seized may be retained for so long as is necessary in all the circumstances but the person in occupation of the premises in question shall be given a copy of anything that is seized if he so requests and the person executing the warrant considers that it can be done without undue delay.

Matters exempt from inspection and seizure

8.　The powers of inspection and seizure conferred by a warrant issued under this Schedule shall not be exercisable in respect of information which is exempt information by virtue of section 23(1) or 24(1).

9.—(1)   Subject to the provisions of this paragraph, the powers of inspection and seizure conferred by a warrant issued under this Schedule shall not be exercisable in respect of—

    (a)   any communication between a professional legal adviser and his client in connection with the giving of legal advice to the client with respect to his obligations, liabilities or rights under this Act, or

    (b)   any communication between a professional legal adviser and his client, or between such an adviser or his client and any other person, made in connection with or in contemplation of proceedings under or arising out of this Act (including proceedings before the Tribunal) and for the purposes of such proceedings.

  (2)   Sub-paragraph (1) applies also to—

    (a)   any copy or other record of any such communication as is there mentioned, and

    (b)   any document or article enclosed with or referred to in any such communication if made in connection with the giving of any advice or, as the case may be, in connection with or in contemplation of and for the purposes of such proceedings as are there mentioned.

  (3)   This paragraph does not apply to anything in the possession of any person other than the professional legal adviser or his client or to anything held with the intention of furthering a criminal purpose.

  (4)   In this paragraph references to the client of a professional legal adviser include references to any person representing such a client.

10. If the person in occupation of any premises in respect of which a warrant is issued under this Schedule objects to the inspection or seizure under the warrant of any material on the grounds that it consists partly of matters in respect of which those powers are not exercisable, he shall, if the person executing the warrant so requests, furnish that person with a copy of so much of the material in relation to which the powers are exercisable.

Return of warrants

11. A warrant issued under this Schedule shall be returned to the court from which it was issued—

    (a)   after being executed, or

    (b)   if not executed within the time authorised for its execution;

and the person by whom any such warrant is executed shall make an endorsement on it stating what powers have been exercised by him under the warrant.

Offences

12. Any person who—

    (a)   intentionally obstructs a person in the execution of a warrant issued under this Schedule, or

    (b)   fails without reasonable excuse to give any person executing such a warrant such assistance as he may reasonably require for the execution of the warrant,

is guilty of an offence.

Vessels, vehicles etc

13. In this Schedule "premises" includes any vessel, vehicle, aircraft or hovercraft, and references to the occupier of any premises include references to the person in charge of any vessel, vehicle, aircraft or hovercraft.

Scotland and Northern Ireland

14. In the application of this Schedule to Scotland—
    (a) for any reference to a circuit judge there is substituted a reference to the sheriff, and
    (b) for any reference to information on oath there is substituted a reference to evidence on oath.

15. In the application of this Schedule to Northern Ireland—
    (a) for any reference to a circuit judge there is substituted a reference to a county court judge, and
    (b) for any reference to information on oath there is substituted a reference to a complaint on oath.

Definitions   For "public authority", see s 3(1); for "decision notice", see s 50; for "information notice", see s 51; for "enforcement notice", see s 52; for "the Commissioner", "exempt information", "information" and "the Tribunal" see s 84.
References   See paras 5.32, 5.33.

SCHEDULE 4

Section 61(1)

APPEAL PROCEEDINGS: AMENDMENTS OF SCHEDULE 6 TO DATA PROTECTION ACT 1998

Constitution of Tribunal in national security cases

1. In paragraph 2(1) of Schedule 6 to the Data Protection Act 1998 (constitution of Tribunal in national security cases), at the end there is inserted "or under section 60(1) or (4) of the Freedom of Information Act 2000".

2. For paragraph 3 of that Schedule there is substituted—

    "3 The Tribunal shall be duly constituted—
        (a) for an appeal under section 28(4) or (6) in any case where the application of paragraph 6(1) is excluded by rules under paragraph 7, or
        (b) for an appeal under section 60(1) or (4) of the Freedom of Information Act 2000,

    if it consists of three of the persons designated under paragraph 2(1), of whom one shall be designated by the Lord Chancellor to preside."

Constitution of Tribunal in other cases

3.—(1)   Paragraph 4 of that Schedule (constitution of Tribunal in other cases) is amended as follows.

    (2)   After sub-paragraph (1) there is inserted—

    "(1A) Subject to any rules made under paragraph 7, the Tribunal shall be duly constituted for an appeal under section 57(1) or (2) of the Freedom of Information Act 2000 if it consists of—
        (a) the chairman or a deputy chairman (who shall preside), and
        (b) an equal number of the members appointed respectively in accordance with paragraphs (aa) and (bb) of section 6(6)."

    (3)   In sub-paragraph (2), after "(1)" there is inserted "or (1A)".

Rules of procedure

4.—(1)   Paragraph 7 of that Schedule (rules of procedure) is amended as follows.

    (2)   In sub-paragraph (1), for the words from "regulating" onwards there is substituted "regulating—
        (a) the exercise of the rights of appeal conferred—

      (i)   by sections 28(4) and (6) and 48, and

     (ii)   by sections 57(1) and (2) and section 60(1) and (4) of the Freedom of Information Act 2000, and

   (b) the practice and procedure of the Tribunal."

(3)   In sub-paragraph (2), after paragraph (a) there is inserted—

"(aa) for the joinder of any other person as a party to any proceedings on an appeal under the Freedom of Information Act 2000,

 (ab) for the hearing of an appeal under this Act with an appeal under the Freedom of Information Act 2000,".

References   See para 5.47.

SCHEDULE 5

Section 67

AMENDMENTS OF PUBLIC RECORDS LEGISLATION

PART I
AMENDMENTS OF PUBLIC RECORDS ACT 1958

Functions of Advisory Council on Public Records

1. In section 1 of the Public Records Act 1958 (general responsibility of the Lord Chancellor for public records), after subsection (2) there is inserted—

"(2A)The matters on which the Advisory Council on Public Records may advise the Lord Chancellor include matters relating to the application of the Freedom of Information Act 2000 to information contained in public records which are historical records within the meaning of Part VI of that Act."

Access to public records

2.—(1)   Section 5 of that Act (access to public records) is amended in accordance with this paragraph.

(2)   Subsections (1) and (2) are omitted.

(3)   For subsection (3) there is substituted—

"(3) It shall be the duty of the Keeper of Public Records to arrange that reasonable facilities are available to the public for inspecting and obtaining copies of those public records in the Public Record Office which fall to be disclosed in accordance with the Freedom of Information Act 2000."

(4)   Subsection (4) and, in subsection (5), the words from "and subject to" to the end are omitted.

3. Schedule 2 of that Act (enactments prohibiting disclosure of information obtained from the public) is omitted.

Power to extend meaning of "public records"

4. In Schedule 1 to that Act (definition of public records) after the Table at the end of paragraph 3 there is inserted—

"3A.—(1)   Her Majesty may by Order in Council amend the Table at the end of paragraph 3 of this Schedule by adding to either Part of the Table an entry relating to any body or establishment—

   (a) which, at the time when the Order is made, is specified in Schedule 2 to the Parliamentary Commissioner Act 1967 (departments, etc subject to investigation), or

   (b) in respect of which an entry could, at that time, be added to Schedule 2 to that Act by an Order in Council under section 4 of that Act (which confers power to amend that Schedule).

(2)　An Order in Council under this paragraph may relate to a specified body or establishment or to bodies or establishments falling within a specified description.

(3)　An Order in Council under this paragraph shall be subject to annulment in pursuance of a resolution of either House of Parliament."

PART II

AMENDMENT OF PUBLIC RECORDS ACT (NORTHERN IRELAND) 1923

5. After section 5 of the Public Records Act (Northern Ireland) 1923 (deposit of documents in Record Office by trustees or other persons) there is inserted—

"5A Access to public records

It shall be the duty of the Deputy Keeper of the Records of Northern Ireland to arrange that reasonable facilities are available to the public for inspecting and obtaining copies of those public records in the Public Record Office of Northern Ireland which fall to be disclosed in accordance with the Freedom of Information Act 2000."

SCHEDULE 6

Section 73

FURTHER AMENDMENTS OF DATA PROTECTION ACT 1998

Request by data controller for further information

1. In section 7 of the Data Protection Act 1998 (right of access to personal data), for subsection (3) there is substituted—

"(3)　Where a data controller—
(a) reasonably requires further information in order to satisfy himself as to the identity of the person making a request under this section and to locate the information which that person seeks, and
(b) has informed him of that requirement,

the data controller is not obliged to comply with the request unless he is supplied with that further information."

Parliament

2. After section 35 of that Act there is inserted—

"35A Parliamentary privilege

Personal data are exempt from—
(a) the first data protection principle, except to the extent to which it requires compliance with the conditions in Schedules 2 and 3,
(b) the second, third, fourth and fifth data protection principles,
(c) section 7, and
(d) sections 10 and 14(1) to (3),

if the exemption is required for the purpose of avoiding an infringement of the privileges of either House of Parliament."

3. After section 63 of that Act there is inserted—

"63A Application to Parliament

(1)　Subject to the following provisions of this section and to section 35A, this Act applies to the processing of personal data by or on behalf of either House of Parliament as it applies to the processing of personal data by other persons.

(2)　Where the purposes for which and the manner in which any personal data are, or are to be, processed are determined by or on behalf of the House of Commons, the data controller in respect of those data for the purposes of this Act shall be the Corporate Officer of that House.

(3)   Where the purposes for which and the manner in which any personal data are, or are to be, processed are determined by or on behalf of the House of Lords, the data controller in respect of those data for the purposes of this Act shall be the Corporate Officer of that House.

(4)   Nothing in subsection (2) or (3) is to be taken to render the Corporate Officer of the House of Commons or the Corporate Officer of the House of Lords liable to prosecution under this Act, but section 55 and paragraph 12 of Schedule 9 shall apply to a person acting on behalf of either House as they apply to any other person."

4. In Schedule 2 to that Act (conditions relevant for the purposes of the first data protection principle: processing of any personal data) in paragraph 5 after paragraph (a) there is inserted—

"(aa) for the exercise of any functions of either House of Parliament,".

5. In Schedule 3 to that Act (conditions relevant for the purposes of the first data protection principle: processing of sensitive personal data) in paragraph 7 after paragraph (a) there is inserted—

"(aa) for the exercise of any functions of either House of Parliament,".

Honours

6. In Schedule 7 to that Act (miscellaneous exemptions) in paragraph 3(b) (honours) after "honour" there is inserted "or dignity".

Legal professional privilege

7. In paragraph 10 of that Schedule (legal professional privilege), for the words "or, in Scotland, to confidentiality as between client and professional legal adviser," there is substituted "or, in Scotland, to confidentiality of communications".

Extension of transitional exemption

8. In Schedule 14 to that Act (transitional provisions), in paragraph 2(1) (which confers transitional exemption from the prohibition on processing without registration on those registered under the Data Protection Act 1984) the words "or, if earlier, 24th October 2001" are omitted.

Definitions   For "data" and "personal data", see the Data Protection Act 1998, s 1(1), as amended (definition "data") by s 68(1), (2)(a); for "data controller", see s 1(1), (4) of that Act.

SCHEDULE 7

Section 76(2)

DISCLOSURE OF INFORMATION BY OMBUDSMEN

The Parliamentary Commissioner for Administration

1. At the end of section 11 of the Parliamentary Commissioner Act 1967 (provision for secrecy of information) there is inserted—

"(5) Information obtained from the Information Commissioner by virtue of section 76(1) of the Freedom of Information Act 2000 shall be treated for the purposes of subsection (2) of this section as obtained for the purposes of an investigation under this Act and, in relation to such information, the reference in paragraph (a) of that subsection to the investigation shall have effect as a reference to any investigation."

2. After section 11A of that Act there is inserted—

"11AA Disclosure of information by Parliamentary Commissioner to Information Commissioner

(1)   The Commissioner may disclose to the Information Commissioner any information obtained by, or furnished to, the Commissioner under or for the purposes of this Act if the information appears to the Commissioner to relate to—

  (a) a matter in respect of which the Information Commissioner could exercise any power conferred by—

  (i)   Part V of the Data Protection Act 1998 (enforcement),

  (ii)   section 48 of the Freedom of Information Act 2000 (practice recommendations), or

  (iii)   Part IV of that Act (enforcement), or

  (b) the commission of an offence under—

  (i)   any provision of the Data Protection Act 1998 other than paragraph 12 of Schedule 9 (obstruction of execution of warrant), or

  (ii)   section 77 of the Freedom of Information Act 2000 (offence of altering etc records with intent to prevent disclosure).

(2)   Nothing in section 11(2) of this Act shall apply in relation to the disclosure of information in accordance with this section."

The Commissions for Local Administration in England and Wales

3. In section 32 of the Local Government Act 1974 (law of defamation, and disclosure of information) after subsection (6) there is inserted—

"(7)   Information obtained from the Information Commissioner by virtue of section 76 of the Freedom of Information Act 2000 shall be treated for the purposes of subsection (2) above as obtained for the purposes of an investigation under this Part of this Act and, in relation to such information, the reference in paragraph (a) of that subsection to the investigation shall have effect as a reference to any investigation."

4. After section 33 of that Act there is inserted—

"33A Disclosure of information by Local Commissioner to Information Commissioner

(1)   A Local Commissioner may disclose to the Information Commissioner any information obtained by, or furnished to, the Local Commissioner under or for the purposes of this Part of this Act if the information appears to the Local Commissioner to relate to—

  (a) a matter in respect of which the Information Commissioner could exercise any power conferred by—

  (i)   Part V of the Data Protection Act 1998 (enforcement),

  (ii)   section 48 of the Freedom of Information Act 2000 (practice recommendations), or

  (iii)   Part IV of that Act (enforcement), or

  (b) the commission of an offence under—

  (i)   any provision of the Data Protection Act 1998 other than paragraph 12 of Schedule 9 (obstruction of execution of warrant), or

  (ii)   section 77 of the Freedom of Information Act 2000 (offence of altering etc records with intent to prevent disclosure).

(2)   Nothing in section 32(2) of this Act shall apply in relation to the disclosure of information in accordance with this section."

The Health Service Commissioners

5. At the end of section 15 of the Health Service Commissioners Act 1993 (confidentiality of information) there is inserted—

"(4) Information obtained from the Information Commissioner by virtue of section 76 of the Freedom of Information Act 2000 shall be treated for the purposes of subsection (1) as obtained for the purposes of an investigation and, in relation to such information, the reference in paragraph (a) of that subsection to the investigation shall have effect as a reference to any investigation."

6. After section 18 of that Act there is inserted—

"18A Disclosure of information to Information Commissioner

(1)   The Health Service Commissioner for England or the Health Service Commissioner for Wales may disclose to the Information Commissioner any information obtained by, or furnished to, the Health Service Commissioner under or for the purposes of this Act if the information appears to the Health Service Commissioner to relate to—

    (a) a matter in respect of which the Information Commissioner could exercise any power conferred by—
        (i)   Part V of the Data Protection Act 1998 (enforcement),
        (ii) section 48 of the Freedom of Information Act 2000 (practice recommendations), or
        (iii) Part IV of that Act (enforcement), or
    (b) the commission of an offence under—
        (i)   any provision of the Data Protection Act 1998 other than paragraph 12 of Schedule 9 (obstruction of execution of warrant), or
        (ii) section 77 of the Freedom of Information Act 2000 (offence of altering etc records with intent to prevent disclosure).

(3)   Nothing in section 15 (confidentiality of information) applies in relation to the disclosure of information in accordance with this section."

The Welsh Administration Ombudsman

7. In Schedule 9 to the Government of Wales Act 1998 (the Welsh Administration Ombudsman), at the end of paragraph 25 (confidentiality of information) there is inserted—

"(5) Information obtained from the Information Commissioner by virtue of section 76 of the Freedom of Information Act 2000 shall be treated for the purposes of sub-paragraph (1) as obtained for the purposes of an investigation and, in relation to such information, the reference in paragraph (a) of that subsection to the investigation shall have effect as a reference to any investigation."

8. After paragraph 27 of that Schedule there is inserted—

"Disclosure of information to Information Commissioner

28.—(1)   The Welsh Administration Ombudsman may disclose to the Information Commissioner any information obtained by, or furnished to, the Welsh Administration Ombudsman under or for the purposes of this Schedule if the information appears to the Welsh Administration Ombudsman to relate to—

    (a) a matter in respect of which the Information Commissioner could exercise any power conferred by—
        (i)   Part V of the Data Protection Act 1998 (enforcement),
        (ii) section 48 of the Freedom of Information Act 2000 (practice recommendations), or
        (iii) Part IV of that Act (enforcement), or

(b) the commission of an offence under—

   (i) any provision of the Data Protection Act 1998 other than paragraph 12 of Schedule 9 (obstruction of execution of warrant), or

   (ii) section 77 of the Freedom of Information Act 2000 (offence of altering etc records with intent to prevent disclosure).

(2) Nothing in paragraph 25(1) applies in relation to the disclosure of information in accordance with this paragraph."

The Northern Ireland Commissioner for Complaints

9. At the end of Article 21 of the Commissioner for Complaints (Northern Ireland) Order 1996 (disclosure of information by Commissioner) there is inserted—

"(5) Information obtained from the Information Commissioner by virtue of section 76 of the Freedom of Information Act 2000 shall be treated for the purposes of paragraph (1) as obtained for the purposes of an investigation under this Order and, in relation to such information, the reference in paragraph (1)(a) to the investigation shall have effect as a reference to any investigation."

10. After that Article there is inserted—

"21A Disclosure of information to Information Commissioner

(1) The Commissioner may disclose to the Information Commissioner any information obtained by, or furnished to, the Commissioner under or for the purposes of this Order if the information appears to the Commissioner to relate to—

   (a) a matter in respect of which the Information Commissioner could exercise any power conferred by—

      (i) Part V of the Data Protection Act 1998 (enforcement),

      (ii) section 48 of the Freedom of Information Act 2000 (practice recommendations), or

      (iii) Part IV of that Act (enforcement), or

   (b) the commission of an offence under—

      (i) any provision of the Data Protection Act 1998 other than paragraph 12 of Schedule 9 (obstruction of execution of warrant), or

      (ii) section 77 of the Freedom of Information Act 2000 (offence of altering etc records with intent to prevent disclosure).

(2) Nothing in Article 21(1) applies in relation to the disclosure of information in accordance with this Article."

The Assembly Ombudsman for Northern Ireland

11. At the end of Article 19 of the Ombudsman (Northern Ireland) Order 1996 there is inserted—

"(5) Information obtained from the Information Commissioner by virtue of section 76 of the Freedom of Information Act 2000 shall be treated for the purposes of paragraph (1) as obtained for the purposes of an investigation under this Order and, in relation to such information, the reference in paragraph (1)(a) to the investigation shall have effect as a reference to any investigation."

12. After that Article there is inserted—

"19A Disclosure of information to Information Commissioner

(1) The Ombudsman may disclose to the Information Commissioner any information obtained by, or furnished to, the Omubudsman under or for the purposes of this Order if the information appears to the Ombudsman to relate to—

(a) a matter in respect of which the Information Commissioner could exercise any power conferred by—
  (i) Part V of the Data Protection Act 1998 (enforcement),
  (ii) section 48 of the Freedom of Information Act 2000 (practice recommendations), or
  (iii) Part IV of that Act (enforcement), or
(b) the commission of an offence under—
  (i) any provision of the Data Protection Act 1998 other than paragraph 12 of Schedule 9 (obstruction of execution of warrant), or
  (ii) section 77 of the Freedom of Information Act 2000 (offence of altering etc records with intent to prevent disclosure).

(2) Nothing in Article 19(1) applies in relation to the disclosure of information in accordance with this Article."

The Commissioner for Local Administration in Scotland

13. In section 30 of the Local Government (Scotland) Act 1975 (limitation on disclosure of information), after subsection (5) there is inserted—

"(5A) Information obtained from the Information Commissioner by virtue of section 76 of the Freedom of Information Act 2000 shall be treated for the purposes of subsection (2) as obtained for the purposes of an investigation under this Part of this Act and, in relation to such information, the reference in subsection (2)(a) to the investigation shall have effect as a reference to any investigation."

References See para 6.11.

SCHEDULE 8
REPEALS

Section 86

PART I
REPEAL COMING INTO FORCE ON PASSING OF ACT

Chapter	Short title	Extent of repeal
1998 c 29	The Data Protection Act 1998	In Schedule 14, in paragraph 2(1), the words "or, if earlier, 24th October 2001".

PART II
REPEALS COMING INTO FORCE IN ACCORDANCE WITH SECTION 87(2)

Chapter	Short title	Extent of repeal
1958 c 51	The Public Records Act 1958	In Schedule 1, in Part II of the Table in paragraph 3, the entry relating to the Data Protection Commissioner.
1967 c 13	The Parliamentary Commissioner Act 1967	In Schedule 2, the entry relating to the Data Protection Commissioner.
1975 c 24	The House of Commons Disqualification Act 1975	In Schedule 1, in Part III, the entry relating to the Data Protection Commissioner.
1975 c 25	The Northern Ireland Assembly Disqualification Act 1975	In Schedule 1, in Part III, the entry relating to the Data Protection Commissioner.
1998 c 29	The Data Protection Act 1998	In Schedule 5, Part III.
		In Schedule 15, paragraphs 1(1), 2, 4, 5(2) and 6(2).

PART III
REPEALS COMING INTO FORCE IN ACCORDANCE WITH SECTION 87(3)

Chapter	Short title	Extent of repeal
1958 c 51	The Public Records Act 1958	In section 5, subsections (1), (2) and (4) and, in subsection (5), the words from "and subject to" to the end. Schedule 2.
1975 c 24	The House of Commons Disqualification Act 1975	In Schedule 1, in Part II, the entry relating to the Data Protection Tribunal.
1975 c 25	The Northern Ireland Assembly Disqualification Act 1975	In Schedule 1, in Part II, the entry relating to the Data Protection Tribunal.
1998 c 29	The Data Protection Act 1998	In section 1(1), in the definition of "data", the word "or" at the end of paragraph (c). In Schedule 15, paragraphs 1(2) and (3), 3, 5(1) and 6(1).

Freedom of Information Act 2000 (Commencement No 1) Order 2001

(SI 2001/1637)

Made   30 April 2001.
Authority   Freedom of Information Act 2000, s 87(3).

1   This Order may be cited as the Freedom of Information Act 2000 (Commencement No 1) Order 2001.

2   The following provisions of the Freedom of Information Act 2000 shall come into force on 14th May 2001:

    (a)   section 18(2), (3), (5), (6) and (7);

    (b)   paragraphs 1(2), 3(2), 5, 8(1), 9(1), 11, 12, 13(3), 14(b), 15(3) and 16 of Schedule 2 (and section 18(4) so far as relating to those provisions);

    (c)   paragraphs 1 and 4 of Schedule 4 (and section 61 so far as relating to those provisions); and

    (d)   paragraphs 1, 6 and 7 of Schedule 6 (and section 73 so far as relating to those provisions).

Appendix 2

Draft Code of Practice on the discharge of the functions of public authorities under Part I of the Freedom of Information Act 2000

Lord Chancellor's Code of Practice on the Management of Records Under Freedom of Information

Draft Code of Practice on the discharge of the functions of public authorities under Part I of the Freedom of Information Act 2000

This Code of Practice is reproduced as set out on the Lord Chancellor's website www.lcd.gov.uk/foi/dftcp00.htm. The functions of the Secretary of State in relation to the Freedom of Information Act 2000 have been transferred to the Lord Chancellor by the Transfer of Functions (Miscellaneous) Order 2001, SI 2001/3500.

The Secretary of State, after consulting the Information Commissioner, issues the following Code of Practice pursuant to section 45 of the Act.

Laid before Parliament on [ ] pursuant to section 45(5) of the Freedom of Information Act 2000.

I Introduction

1. This code of practice provides guidance to public authorities as to the practice which it would, in the opinion of the Secretary of State, be desirable for them to follow in connection with the discharge of their functions under Part I (Access to Information held by public authorities) of the Freedom of Information Act ("the Act").

2. The aims of the Code are to—
   — facilitate the disclosure of information under the Act by setting out good administrative practice that it is desirable for public authorities to follow when handling requests for information, including, where appropriate, the transfer of a request to a different authority;
   — protect the interests of applicants by setting out standards for the provision of advice which it would be good practice to make available to them and to encourage the development of effective means of complaining about decisions taken under the Act;
   — ensure that the interests of third parties who may be affected by any decision to disclose information are considered by the authority by setting standards for consultation; and
   — ensure that authorities consider the implications for Freedom of Information before agreeing to confidentiality provisions in contracts and accepting information in confidence from a third party more generally.

3. Although there is a statutory duty on the Secretary of State to issue the Code, the provisions of the Code themselves do not have statutory force. The statutory requirements for dealing with requests for information are contained in the Act and regulations made under it and public authorities must comply with these statutory provisions at all times. However, section 47 of the Act places a duty on the Information Commissioner to promote the following of good practice by public authorities ("good practice" includes compliance with the provisions of the Code), and section 48 of the Act enables the Information Commissioner to issue a "practice recommendation" to a public authority if it appears to him that the practice of the authority does not conform with that proposed in the Code. Further, section 16 of the Act places a duty on public

authorities to provide advice and assistance to applicants and potential applicants. Authorities will have complied with this duty in any particular case if they have conformed with the Code in relation to the provision of advice or assistance in that case.

4. Words and expressions used in this Code have the same meaning as the same words and expressions used in the Act.

II The provision of advice to persons making requests for information

5. Every public authority should provide advice and assistance (as set out below) to those who propose to make, or who have made, requests for information to it, in order to facilitate their use of the Act.

6. Public authorities should publish their procedures for dealing with requests for information, which should include an address (including an e-mail address where possible) to which applicants may direct requests for information or for assistance. These procedures should be referred to in the authority's publication scheme.

7. A request for information must be made in writing (which includes a request transmitted by electronic means which is received in legible form and is capable of being used for subsequent reference). Where a person is unable to frame their request in writing, the public authority should ensure that appropriate assistance is given to enable that person to make a request for information. Appropriate assistance could include—

— advising the person that another person or agency (such as a Citizens Advice Bureau) can assist them with the application, or make the application on their behalf;

— offering to take a note of the application over the telephone and then send the note to the applicant for confirmation (in which case the written note of the telephone request, once verified by the applicant and returned, would constitute a written request for information and the statutory time limit for reply would begin when the written confirmation was received).

8. Where insufficient information is provided by the applicant to enable the authority to identify and locate the information sought or the request is ambiguous, the authority should, as far as practicable, provide assistance to the applicant to enable him to describe more clearly the information requested. The aim of such assistance is to clarify the nature of the information sought, not to determine the aims or motivation of the applicant. Appropriate assistance could include—

— the provision of an outline of the different kinds of information which might meet the terms of the request;

— the provision of detailed catalogues and indexes, where these are available, to help the applicant ascertain the nature and extent of the information held by the authority;

— the provision of a general response to the request setting out options for further information which could be provided on request;

— where a request would be refused on cost grounds an indication of what information could be provided within the cost ceiling.

9. If, following the provision of such assistance, the applicant has failed to describe the information requested in a way which would enable the authority to identify and locate it, the authority is not expected to seek further clarification, though it must disclose any information relating to the application, which has been successfully identified and found, and which is disclosable under the provisions of the Act, and should explain to the applicant why it cannot take the request any further.

10. An authority cannot seek information from an applicant which he cannot reasonably be expected to possess, such as a file reference number, or a description of a particular record, unless this information is made available by the authority for the use of applicants.

11. An authority is not expected to provide assistance to applicants whose requests are vexatious within the meaning of section 14 of the Act.

III Timeliness in dealing with requests for information where the public interest must be considered

12. Where a public authority needs to consider where the public interest lies in respect of an application for exempt information, although there is no statutory time limit on the length of time the authority may take to reach its decision, it must, under section 17(2), give an estimate of the date by which it expects to reach such a decision. Authorities are expected to give estimates which are reasonable in the circumstances of the particular case, and they are expected to comply with their estimates in the majority of cases.

13. Public authorities should aim to make <u>all</u> decisions within 20 working days, wherever possible.

IV Transferring requests for information

14. Where a public authority receives a request for information which it does not hold, within the meaning of section 3(2) of the Act, but which it believes is held by another public authority, it should consider whether it should consult that authority with a view to ascertaining whether it does hold the information and, if so, whether it should transfer the request to it. If the request is for information some of which is held by the authority and some of which is not, the provisions in respect of transfer of requests in the code only apply to that part of the request which relates to information which the authority does not hold.

15. The process of consulting another authority does not relieve the first authority of its obligations under the Act to advise the applicant that it does not hold the information (or part of it). It should consider whether it is appropriate at that stage to inform the applicant that the information is held by the other authority and, if it does so inform him, to ask him whether he wants the request transferred.

16. Before transferring a request for information to another authority, the authority should consider—
— whether a transfer is possible;
— if it is, it should consider whether the applicant would have any grounds to object to the transfer;

— if the authority reasonably concludes that the applicant would not object, it may transfer without going back to the applicant, but should tell him it has done so (as well as complying with its obligations under the Act);

— in any case where there are reasonable grounds to believe an applicant will object, the authority should only transfer with his consent.

17. The authority receiving the initial request must always disclose such information relating to the request as it holds, before transferring a request to another authority. A request or part of a request transferred to another public authority, with the agreement of that authority, would be a request within the meaning of the Act to that authority. Consequently the receiving authority must comply with its obligations under Part I of the Act in the same way as it would for a request which is received direct from an applicant.

18. All transfers of requests should take place promptly.

19. Where a public authority is unable to facilitate the transfer of a request for information to another authority or considers it inappropriate to do so, it should consider what advice, if any, it can provide to the applicant to enable him to pursue his request.

20. When a request for information has been transferred to another authority, with the agreement of the receiving authority, the first authority has no further responsibility for handling the request.

V Consultation with third parties

21. In some cases the disclosure of information pursuant to a request may affect the legal rights of a third party such as the right to have certain information treated in confidence or rights under Article 8 of the European Convention on Human Rights. Where the consent of the third party would enable a disclosure to be made an authority should consult that party prior to reaching a decision, unless it is clear to the authority that the consent would not be forthcoming.

22. Where the interests of the third party which may be affected by a disclosure do not give rise to legal rights, the public authority should consider whether it should consult the third party.

Consultation will be unnecessary where—

— the public authority does not intend to disclose the information relying on some other legitimate ground;

— the views of the third party can have no effect on the decision of the authority, for example, where there is other legislation preventing or requiring the disclosure of this information; or

A public authority may consider that consultation is not appropriate where the cost of consulting with third parties would be disproportionate.

23. Consultation should take place where—

— the views of the third party may assist the authority to determine whether information is exempt from disclosure under the Act; or

— the views of the third party may assist the authority to determine where the public interest lies under section 2 of the Act.

24. Where the interests (but not the legal rights) of a number of third parties may be affected by a disclosure and those parties have a representative organisation which can express views on behalf of those parties, the authority may, if it considers consultation appropriate, consider that it would be sufficient to consult that representative organisation. If there is no representative organisation, the authority may consider that it would be sufficient to consult a representative sample of the third parties in question.

25. The fact that the third party has not responded to consultation does not relieve the authority of its duty to disclose information under the Act, or its duty to reply within the time specified in the Act.

VI Freedom of information and public sector contracts

26. When entering into contracts public authorities should refuse to include contractual terms which purport to restrict the disclosure of information held by the authority and relating to the contract beyond the restrictions permitted by the Act. Public authorities should not agree to hold information 'in confidence' which is not in fact confidential in nature.

27. When entering into contracts with non-public authority contractors, public authorities may be under pressure to accept confidentiality clauses so that information relating to the terms of the contract, its value and performance will be exempt from disclosure. Public authorities should not accept such clauses where this is commercially viable.

28. Any acceptance of such confidentiality provisions must be for good reasons and capable of being justified to the Commissioner.

29. Except where paragraph 30 below applies, it is for the public authority to disclose information pursuant to the Act, and not the contractor. However, the public authority may need to protect from disclosure by the contractor information which would be exempt from disclosure under the Act, by appropriate contractual terms. Apart from such cases, public authorities should not impose terms of secrecy on contractors.

VII Accepting information in confidence from third parties

30. A public authority should only accept information from third parties in confidence if it is necessary to obtain that information in connection with the exercise of any of the authority's functions. In addition, public authorities should not agree to hold information received from third parties 'in confidence' which is not confidential in nature. And again, acceptance of any confidentiality provisions must be for good reasons, capable of being justified to the Commissioner.

VIII Complaints procedure

31. All public authorities should have in place a procedure for dealing with complaints from people who consider that their request has not been properly handled, or who are otherwise dissatisfied with the outcome of the consideration of their request, and the issue cannot be resolved in discussion with the official dealing with the request.

32. When communicating any decision made in relation to a request under the Act, public authorities should provide details of their complaints procedure, including how to make a complaint.

33. The complaints procedure should be a fair and impartial means of dealing with handling problems and reviewing decisions taken pursuant to the Act, including decisions taken about where the public interest lies in respect of exempt information. It should be possible to reverse or otherwise amend decisions previously taken. Complaints procedures should be clear and should be capable of producing a prompt determination of the complaint.

35. Where practicable, complaints procedures should be handled by a person who was not a party to the original decision.

36. In all cases, the complainant should be informed of the outcome of his complaint.

37. The public authority should publish target times for determining complaints and information as to how successful it is with meeting those targets. Records should be kept of all complaints and of their outcome. Authorities should have procedures in place for monitoring complaints and for reviewing, and, if necessary, amending, policies where such action is indicated by regular reversals of initial decisions.

38. Where the outcome of a complaint is that information should be disclosed which was previously withheld, the information in question should be disclosed as soon as practicable.

39. Where the outcome of a complaint is that the procedures within an authority have not been properly followed by an individual within an authority, the authority should apologise to the applicant and take appropriate steps to reduce the likelihood of errors of this type occurring in future.

40. Where the outcome of a complaint is that an initial decision to withhold information is upheld, or is otherwise in the authority's favour, the applicant should be informed of his right to apply to the Commissioner, and be given details of how to make an application, for a decision whether the request for information has been dealt with in accordance with the requirements of Part I of the Act.

Lord Chancellor's Code of Practice on the Management of Records Under Freedom of Information

CODE OF PRACTICE ON (1) THE MANAGEMENT OF RECORDS BY PUBLIC AUTHORITIES AND (2) THE TRANSFER AND REVIEW OF PUBLIC RECORDS UNDER THE FREEDOM OF INFORMATION ACT 2000

This Code of Practice (Version 23, 18 January 2001) is reproduced as set out on the Public Record Office website www.pro.gov.uk/recordsmanagement/codeofpractice.htm.

The Lord Chancellor, after consulting the Secretary of State for the Home Department and the Information Commissioner, issues the following Code of Practice pursuant to section 46 of the Freedom of Information Act.

Laid before Parliament on [ ] pursuant to section 46(6) of the Freedom of Information Act 2000.

INTRODUCTION

1. The aims of the Code are—

(1) to set out practices which public authorities and bodies subject to the Public Records Act 1958 and the Public Records Act (NI) 1923 should follow in relation to the creation, keeping, management and destruction of their records (Part One of the Code), and

(2) to describe the arrangements which public record bodies should follow in reviewing public records and transferring them to the Public Record Office or to places of deposit or to the Public Record Office of Northern Ireland (Part Two of the Code)

2. This Code refers to records in all technical or physical formats.

3. Part One of the Code provides a framework for the management of records of public authorities and bodies subject to the Public Records Act 1958 and the Public Records Act (NI) 1923, and Part Two deals with the transfer and review of public records. More detailed guidance on both themes may be obtained from published standards. Those which support the objectives of this Code most directly are listed at Annex A.

4. Words and expressions used in this Code have the same meaning as the same words and expressions used in the FOIA.

PART ONE: RECORDS MANAGEMENT

5. Functional Responsibility

5.1 The records management function should be recognised as a specific corporate programme within an authority and should receive the necessary levels of organisational support to ensure effectiveness. It should bring together responsibilities for records in all formats, including electronic records, throughout their life cycle, from planning and creation through to ultimate disposal. It should have clearly defined responsibilities and objectives, and the resources to achieve them. It is desirable that the person, or persons, responsible for the records management function should also have either direct responsibility or an organisational connection with the person or persons responsible for freedom of information, data protection and other information management issues.

6. Policy

6.1 An authority should have in place an overall policy statement, endorsed by top management and made readily available to staff at all levels of the organisation, on how it manages its records, including electronic records.

6.2 This policy statement should provide a mandate for the performance of all records and information management functions. In particular, it should set out an authority's commitment to create, keep and manage records which document its principal activities. The policy should also outline the role of records management and its relationship to the authority's overall strategy; define roles and responsibilities including the responsibility of individuals to document their actions and decisions in the authority's records, and to dispose of records; provide a framework for supporting standards, procedures and guidelines; and indicate the way in which compliance with the policy and its supporting standards, procedures and guidelines will be monitored.

6.3 The policy statement should be reviewed at regular intervals (at least once every three years) and, if appropriate, amended to maintain its relevance.

7. Human Resources

7.1 A designated member of staff of appropriate seniority should have lead responsibility for records management within the authority. This lead role should be formally acknowledged and made known throughout the authority.

7.2 Staff responsible for records management should have the appropriate skills and knowledge needed to achieve the aims of the records management programme. Responsibility for all aspects of record keeping should be specifically defined and incorporated in the role descriptions or similar documents.

7.3 Human resource policies and practices in organisations should address the need to recruit and retain good quality staff and should accordingly support the records management function in the following areas—

— the provision of appropriate resources to enable the records management function to be maintained across all of its activities;

— the establishment and maintenance of a scheme, such as a competency framework, to identify the knowledge, skills and corporate competencies required in records and information management;

— the regular review of selection criteria for records management posts to ensure currency and compliance with best practice;

— the regular analysis of training needs;

— the establishment of a professional development programme for records management staff;

— the inclusion in induction training programmes for all new staff of an awareness of records issues and practices.

8. Active Records Management

Record Creation

8.1 Each operational/business unit of an authority should have in place an adequate system for documenting its activities. This system should take into account the legislative and regulatory environments in which the authority works.

8.2 Records of a business activity should be complete and accurate enough to allow employees and their successors to undertake appropriate actions in the context of their responsibilities, to—

— facilitate an audit or examination of the business by anyone so authorised,

— protect the legal and other rights of the authority, its clients and any other person affected by its actions, and

— provide authenticity of the records so that the evidence derived from them is shown to be credible and authoritative.

8.3 Records created by the authority should be arranged in a record keeping system that will enable the authority to obtain the maximum benefit from the quick and easy retrieval of information.

Record Keeping

8.4 A prerequisite for achieving effective record keeping systems is the information survey or record audit. This gives an objective view of an authority's records and their relationships to organisational functions, it helps to determine what is required to install and maintain a records management programme, and promotes control of the records.

8.5 Paper and electronic record keeping systems should contain metadata (descriptive and technical documentation) to enable the system and the records to be understood and to be operated efficiently, and to provide an administrative context for effective management of the records.

8.6 The record-keeping system, whether paper or electronic, should include a set of rules for referencing, titling, indexing and, if appropriate, security marking of records. These should be easily understood and should enable the efficient retrieval of information.

Record Maintenance

8.7 A tracking system should be used to control the movement and location of records. This should be sufficient to ensure that a record can be easily retrieved at any time, that any outstanding issues can be dealt with, and that there is an auditable trail of record transactions.

8.8 Storage accommodation for current records must be clean and tidy, and it should prevent damage to the records. Equipment used for current records should provide storage which is safe from unauthorised access and which meets fire regulations, but which allows maximum accessibility to the information commensurate with its frequency of use. When records are no longer required for the conduct of current business, their placement in a designated records centre rather than in offices is a more economical and efficient way to store them. Procedures for handling records should take full account of the need to preserve important information.

8.9 A contingency or business recovery plan should be in place to provide protection for records which are vital to the continued functioning of the authority.

9. Disposal Arrangements

9.1 It is particularly important under FOI that the disposal of records—which is here defined as the point in their lifecycle when they are either transferred to an archives or destroyed—is undertaken in accordance with clearly established policies which have been formally adopted by authorities and which are enforced by properly authorised staff.

Record Closure

9.2   Records must be closed as soon as they have ceased to be of active use other than for reference purposes. As a general rule, files should be closed after five years and, if action continues, a further file should be opened. An indication that a file of paper records or folder of electronic records has been closed should be shown on the record itself as well as noted in the index or database of the files/folders. Wherever possible, information on the intended disposal of electronic records should be included in the metadata when the record is created.

9.3   The storage of closed records awaiting disposal should follow accepted standards relating to environment, security and physical organisation.

Appraisal Planning and Documentation

9.4   In order to make their disposal policies work effectively and for those to which the FOIA applies to provide the information required under FOI legislation, authorities need to have in place systems for managing appraisal and for recording the disposal decisions made. An assessment of the volume and nature of records due for disposal, the time taken to appraise records, and the risks associated with destruction or delay in appraisal will provide information to support an authority's resource planning and workflow arrangements.

9.5   An appraisal documentation system will ensure consistency in records appraisal and disposal. It must show what records are designated for destruction, the authority under which they are to be destroyed and when they are to be destroyed. It should also provide background information on the records, such as legislative provisions, functional context and physical arrangement. This information will provide valuable data for placing records selected for preservation into context and will enable future records managers to provide evidence of the operation of their selection policies.

Record Selection

9.6   Each authority should maintain a selection policy which states in broad terms the functions from which records are likely to be selected for permanent preservation and the periods for which other records should be retained. The policy should be supported by or linked to disposal schedules which should cover all records created, including electronic records. Schedules should be arranged on the basis of series or collection and should indicate the appropriate disposal action for all records (e.g. review after x years; destroy after y years).

9.7   Records selected for permanent preservation and no longer in regular use by the authority should be transferred as soon as possible to an archival institution that has adequate storage and public access facilities (see Part Two of this Code for arrangements for bodies subject to the Public Records Acts).

9.8   Records not selected for permanent preservation and which have reached the end of their administrative life should be destroyed in as secure a manner as is necessary for the level of confidentiality or security markings they bear. A record of the destruction of records, showing their reference, description and date of destruction should be maintained and preserved by the records manager. Disposal schedules would constitute the basis of such a record.

9.9   If a record due for destruction is known to be the subject of a request for information, destruction should be delayed until disclosure has taken place or, if the authority has decided not to disclose the information, until the complaint and appeal provisions of the FOIA have been exhausted.

10. Management of Electronic Records

10.1 The principal issues for the management of electronic records are the same as those for the management of any record. They include, for example the creation of authentic records, the tracking of records and disposal arrangements. However, the means by which these issues are addressed in the electronic environment will be different.

10.2 Effective electronic record keeping requires—
— a clear understanding of the nature of electronic records;
— the creation of records and metadata necessary to document business processes: this should be part of the systems which hold the records;
— the maintenance of a structure of folders to reflect logical groupings of records;
— the secure maintenance of the integrity of electronic records;
— the accessibility and use of electronic records for as long as required (which may include their migration across systems);
— the application of appropriate disposal procedures, including procedures for archiving; and
— the ability to cross reference electronic records to their paper counterparts in a mixed environment.

10.3 Generic requirements for electronic record management systems are set out in the 1999 Public Record Office statement Functional Requirements and Testing of Electronic Records Management Systems. (see http//www.pro.gov.uk/recordsmanagement/eros/invest.htm). Authorities are encouraged to use these as a model when developing their specifications for such systems.

10.4 Audit trails should be provided for all electronic information and documents. They should be kept securely and should be available for inspection by authorised personnel. The BSI document Principles of Good Practice for Information Management (PD0010) recommends audits at predetermined intervals for particular aspects of electronic records management.

10.5 Authorities should seek to conform to the provisions of BSI DISC PD0008—A Code of Practice for Legal Admissibility and Evidential Weight of Information Stored Electronically (2nd edn)—especially for those records likely to be required as evidence.

PART TWO: REVIEW AND TRANSFER OF PUBLIC RECORDS

11.1 This part of the Code relates to the arrangements which authorities should follow to ensure the timely and effective review and transfer of public records. Accordingly, it is relevant only to authorities which are subject to the Public Records Acts 1958 and 1967 or to the Public Records Act (NI) 1923. The general purpose of this part of the Code is to facilitate the performance by the Public Record Office, the Public Record Office of Northern Ireland and other public authorities of their functions under the Freedom of Information Act.

11.2 Under the Public Records Acts, records selected for preservation may be transferred either to the Public Record Office or to places of deposit appointed by the Lord Chancellor. This Code applies to all such transfers. For guidance on which records may be transferred to which institution, and on the disposition of UK public records relating to Northern Ireland, see the Public Record Office Acquisition Policy (1998) and the Public Record Office Disposition Policy (2000).

11.3 In reviewing records for public release, authorities should ensure that public records become available to the public at the earliest possible time in accordance with the FOIA.

11.4 Authorities which have created or are otherwise responsible for public records should ensure that they operate effective arrangements to determine—

    (a)   which records should be selected for permanent preservation; and

    (b)   which records should be released to the public.

These arrangements should be established and operated under the supervision of the Public Record Office or, in Northern Ireland, in conjunction with the Public Record Office of Northern Ireland. The objectives and arrangements for the review of records for release are described in greater detail below.

11.5 In carrying out their review of records for release to the public, authorities should observe the following points—

11.5.1 transfer to the Public Record Office must take place by the time the records are 30 years old, unless the Lord Chancellor gives authorisation for them to be retained for a longer period of time (see section 3(4) of the Public Records Act 1958). By agreement with the Public Record Office, transfer and release may take place before 30 years;

11.5.2 review—for selection and release—should therefore take place before the records in question are 30 years old.

11.5.3 in Northern Ireland transfer under the Public Records Act (NI) 1923 to the Public Record Office of Northern Ireland is normally at 20 years.

11.6 In the case of records to be transferred to the Public Record Office or to a place of deposit appointed under section 4 of the Public Records Act 1958, or to the Public Record Office of Northern Ireland, the purpose of the review of records for release to the public is to—

    — consider which information must be available to the public on transfer because no exemptions under the FOIA apply;

    — consider which information must be available to the public at 30 years because relevant exemptions in the FOIA have ceased to apply;

    — consider whether the information must be released in the public interest, notwithstanding the application of an exemption under the FOIA; and

    — consider which information merits continued protection in accordance with the provisions of the FOIA.

11.7 If the review results in the identification of specified information which the authorities consider ought not to be released under the terms of the FOIA, the authorities should prepare a schedule identifying this information precisely, citing the relevant exemption(s), explaining why the information may not be released and identifying a date at which either release would be appropriate or a date at which the case for release should be reconsidered. This schedule must be submitted to the Public Record Office or, in Northern Ireland, to the Public Record Office of Northern Ireland at the time of transfer which must be before the records containing the information are 30 years old (in the case of the Public Record Office) or 20 years old (in the case of the Public Record Office of Northern Ireland). Authorities should consider whether parts of records might be released if the sensitive information were blanked out.

11.8 In the first instance, the schedule described in 11.7 is to be submitted to the Public Record Office for review and advice. The case in favour of withholding the records for a period longer than 30 years is then considered by the Advisory Council. The Advisory Council may respond as follows—

(a) by accepting that the information may be withheld for longer than 30 years and earmarking the records for release or re-review at the date identified by the authority;

(b) by accepting that the information may be withheld for longer than 30 years but asking the authority to reconsider the later date designated for release or re-review;

(c) by questioning the basis on which it is deemed that the information may be withheld for longer than 30 years and asking the authority to reconsider the case;

(d) by advising the Lord Chancellor if it is not satisfied with the responses it receives from authorities on particular cases;

(e) by taking such other action as it deems appropriate within its role as defined in the Public Records Act.

In Northern Ireland there are separate administrative arrangements requiring that schedules are submitted to a Sensitivity Review Group consisting of representatives of different departments. The Sensitivity Review Group has the role of advising public authorities as to the appropriateness or otherwise of releasing records.

11.9 For the avoidance of doubt, none of the actions described in this Code affects the statutory rights of access established under the FOIA. Requests for information in public records transferred to the Public Record Office or to a place of deposit appointed under section 4 of the Public Records Act 1958 or to the Public Record Office of Northern Ireland will be dealt with on a case by case basis in accordance with the provisions of the FOIA.

11.10 Where records are transferred to the Public Record Office or a place of deposit before they are 30 years old, they should be designated by the transferring department or agency for immediate release unless an exemption applies: there will be no formal review of these designations.

11.11 When an exemption has ceased to apply under section 63 of the FOIA the records will become automatically available to researchers on the day specified in the finalised schedule (i.e. the schedule after it has been reviewed by the Advisory Council). In other cases, if the authority concerned wishes further to extend the period during which the information is to be withheld in accordance with the FOIA, it should submit a further schedule explaining the sensitivity of the information. This is to be done before the expiry of the period stated in the earlier schedule. The Public Record Office and Advisory Council will then review the schedule in accordance with the process described in paragraph 11.8 above. In Northern Ireland, Ministerial approval is required for any further extension of the stated period.

11.12 In reviewing records an authority may identify those which are appropriate for retention within the department, after they are 30 years old, under section 3(4) of the Public Records Act 1958. Applications must be submitted to the Public Record Office for review and advice. The case in favour of retention beyond the 30 year period will then be considered by the Advisory Council. The Advisory Council will consider the case for retaining individual records unless there is already in place a standing authorisation by the Lord Chancellor for the retention of a whole category of records. It will consider such applications on the basis of the guidance in chapter 9 of the White Paper Open Government (Cm 2290, 1993) or subsequent revisions of government policy on retention.

ANNEX A

STANDARDS ACCEPTED IN RECORDS MANAGEMENT

International Standards (ISO)

ISO 15489   International Standard on Records Management (in preparation)

British Standards (BSI)

BS 4783 Storage, transportation and maintenance of media for use in data processing and information storage

BS 7799 Code of practice for information security management

BSI DISC PD 0008 Code of practice for legal admissibility and evidential weight of information stored on electronic document management systems

BSI DISC PD0010 Principles of good practice for information management

BSI DISC PD0012 Guide to the practical implications of the Data Protection Act 1998

Public Record Office standards for the management of public records

RMS 1.1 File Creation (1998)

RMS 2.1 Tracking Records (1998)

RMS 3.1 Storage of Semi-Current Records (1999)

RMS 3.2 Business Recovery Plans (2001)

RMS 5.1 Disposal Scheduling (1998)

Management, Appraisal and Preservation of Electronic Records (2 vols), (1999)

Records Management: Human Resources (1999)

Index

.